What reviewers are saying about

Women
Standing Strong
Together©

"Savvy Chef's short, passionate story is more than a tale of love lost. It's about boxing up the old and embracing the new, finding strength in oneself and enjoying life as a party of one. The emotional sensuality of food, beverage and passion is brilliant, the writing hypnotic. I look forward to reading more from this author."

—Karie Engels, Editor and Author of *There is Nothing Here*

"Bonnie lost two very important souls in her life. It was very moving. Her way of bringing you into the moment is truly artistic and I admire it deeply. My heart goes out to their family, and I commend her for sharing this story. It truly resonated with me, and I know it will touch many others as well."

—Omayra Aregullin

"An inspiring story about rediscovering joy through art, amidst the debilitating presence of fear. The last few years brought out many new fears in all of us. Rodine provided us a blessing to read her artists journey of PTSD and her acceptance and reclamation of power."

—Lauren Cadieux

"The author openly shares the struggles of excitement and wonder, turned to sadness and a broken spirit, and further despair and bewilderment from the circumstances that life has thrown at her. But Linda's experiences, she doesn't fill the cracks of brokenness with the scars of defeat, darkness, and shattered dreams. Rather, she reaches out to God, and the rays of light emanating from God's favor and grace begin to shine through those cracks. What results is love, redemption, and a renewed sense of meaning and purpose for life."

–Jonathon Sherrill

"From the beginning, this story took my breath away. A young teen's life is tied up between love and enabling a person to take her heart and smash it. It could have been me and so many other young girls who focus on outside relationships to bring meaning to our lives. When it is finished, the ghost of the relationship controls from the shadows. Irene immerses herself in day-to-day tasks, believing she will never reach her potential. Irene's search for meaning allows her to open herself to God to heal.

–Robin Magaddino, author *Out of the Darkness*

"The loss of innocence is a compelling story as we all have thoughts of what that should look like. Ann Marie shares her soul as she takes you back into time and reopens wounds of lost adolescence while bravely finding a way through many phases of her life to bring her to a place today where she owns herself completely. It's all hers. the fear, pain, depression, wonder, discovery, and strength. She moves from loss of innocence into sharing her passion in life and encourages us as women to embrace all of ourselves, taking the lessons with us and turning them into powerful outcomes."

–Robin Salls, Founder & CEO of *Tangled Silver Magazine*

"Chrisanthi's story is divine, encouraging and emotional. It is a beautifully written piece that will inspire and uplift others, spiritually, physically and mentally overcome any challenges . Her strength and trust in God is encouraging. When faced with any difficult circumstances, we can rise above and overcome anything. She is a true warrior and I look forward to reading more of her work."

–Melissa Barnett

"This is an account of one woman's journey leading out of the shadows of abuse and into the light of transformative healing. In the search for an authentic voice, Dina weaves together past moments of spiritual clarity into a blanket of vocal toning she uses to warm others hearts. This is uplifting, inspirational and triumphant! It leaves the reader wanting more... to hear the mystical vocals that light up the human biofield, connecting earth with heaven. Thank you for a beautiful read."

–Katie Chenoweth, MAEd, LMBT, CHt

"Never again will I risk my life by not taking care of myself first." This is the most powerful statement for me. I feel the candor, honesty, pain, joy, relief & release in the vivid descriptions that make me feel everything the author felt. Margaret was in physical freefalling! This story helps me understand real strength of character. Margaret served others when she needed serving self. She knew God was with her even during intense pain. It takes a special heart, mind, spirit, person, to do all you have accomplished. Your story is powerful, compelling, and grips my heart as I thank God for you coming out on top!"

–Dorma Jean McGruder,
One Bad Decision & Thank God For Closed Doors

"Embracing the gift of empathic intuition isn't always an easy journey. This story is about Judy's initial fright about her intense childhood visions and how she learned to shed her fear and trust her instincts. I am inspired by this journey of personal growth, spiritual understanding and unconditional love and the sharing of her deep wisdom through her unusual experience."

–Karen Carnabucci, LCSW, TEP,
Author of *Show and Tell Psychodrama:*
Skills for Therapists, Coaches, Teachers, Leader

Women Standing Strong Together©

VOLUME II

A Collection of Stories with Soul Purpose

Women Standing Strong Together
Volume II 2023

Copyright© 2023 by Gloria Coppola

Cover Design© Urban Writers
Cover art© Beverly Ash Gilbert
Book Design© Michelle Fairbanks
Editing and Proofreading Patty Pascua
Story Development Coaching Gloria Coppola
Virtual Assistant Teaka Carrassco

ISBN 979-8-9856466-4-1

Printed in the United States of America
First Printing Edition 2023

www.PPP-publishing.com

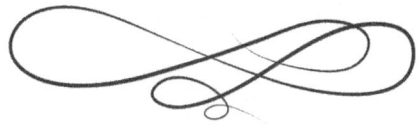

To every woman who shed a tear through life
To every smile that brightened up a room
To every woman who carried you
We celebrate the goddess

–Gloria Coppola

Contents

"There is nothing more rare, nor more beautiful, than a woman being unapologetically herself; comfortable in her perfect imperfection. To me, that is the true essence of beauty."

—DR. STEVE MARABOLI

The authors voice

The uniqueness of every individual comes through their passionate words of expression and their heart. Fourteen women gathered from around the world, all with different backgrounds.

"The drama of life is a psychological one, in which all conditions, circumstances and events of your life are brought to pass by your assumptions. To become the master of your assumptions is the key to undreamed-of-freedom and happiness." Neville Goddard

Everything is connected. This is the message of the ancestors. This is the portal to truth and the way of being in the breath of God's Love. When one creates their story, the vision unfolds in their language and emotions. We are here to listen, to learn, to be inspired and understand there is a thread between us all.

It is my hope you find yourself in several of these stories. To be inspired, knowing you are not alone. To find the perfection in the imperfection of all of life and our own assumptions, therein lies freedom to the expression of your true self.

—GLORIA COPPOLA

A note from the artist

You know who they are – those friends you haven't seen for years – the ones who live in a special place in your heart and who hold a piece of you in theirs. When you get together, conversation and laughter and inside jokes flow. You can be yourself, your REAL self without feeling embarrassed that your belly sticks out a bit more, your wrinkles are deeper and more of your joints ache.

You know who they are – those deep, special friends who love you for who you are on the inside. You feel ALIVE in their presence, energized, as if everything is full of color and light and funny little moments. Your cheeks hurt from smiling and laughing, a few tears flow, and time goes way too quickly.

When was the last time you reached out to get together with those friends you think about, but forget to call? I'm talking about really connecting with the ones who you share that deep bond.

My challenge to you:

Reach out and connect with a friend who you've lost touch with and tell her how much she means to you. Then plan a time to call, to meet-up in some form and spend time together.

Are you still isolating? Or far away from your friend? No problem! One thing I've learned in the last few years – we don't need to breathe the same air in order to connect!

I raise my arms to the moon and send my love to you and your friend(s), *Beverly Ash Gilbert*

Come visit me: BeverlyAshGilbert.com

Linda Rose

I'm the Savvy Chef, someone who loves food as you will tell from my story. I write for the joy of it and have published work in cookbooks and culinary magazines.

Attending food and wine related events internationally is the way I embrace joy in my life. I love diversity and help support promotions and hospitality. It's fun. When I'm not traveling around visiting fine restaurants and kitchens, savouring local cuisines; I'm promoting my blog about the food, wine and hospitality.

You can find me collaborating with a range of partners, chefs, food products and recipe creators internationally. Such a joy to provide promotional services to their food agenda and themes.

Savvy Chef recipes and food blogs are shared on Facebook, Twitter, and Pinterest. Please stop by and find the joy in cooking. As a keen recipe creator and food traveler, I am also working on several international food and wine related initiatives for aspirational leaders in the industry. Perhaps, I shall meet you along the journey one day.

Facebook@SavvyChefLin
Twitter@SavvyChef1
TheSavvyChef@Pinterest
You can reach me at TheSavvyChef@Outlook.com

CHAPTER ONE

Sweet and Sour

LINDA ROSE

We were welcomed like royalty feasting at the Majaraja's City Palace, which sets upon the elegant Lake Pichola, India.

The interior of the castle boasts lavish chambers, crystal chandeliers, unpredictable carvings, large reception halls, and gilded wall decorations. My eyes open wide, my head spinning around to take in the ornate beauty of this delightful palace with a deep sigh.

The royal residence is one of the most distinguished structures of their nation. They feature floats of brilliant-colored flowers in splendid fountains, shimmering blue water of magnificent baths and private pools, doric pillars, ornamental brackets, decorative staircases, and light streaming in through large windows. India possesses some of the most enchanting forts and palaces, a genuine royal retreat. Each place we explored seemed like a magical dream.

Today we would celebrate once again. Lunch consisted of very spicy chicken and vegetables, tantalizing our senses. Every taste more decadent than the next. Love embellished the vibrant kisses on our lips, honoring my birthday, dining in the historic and spectacular outdoor courtyard. The waiters graciously served us like the emperors who came before us, presenting a dessert of spiced malai kulfi ice cream. Imagine that melting on your tongue.

The infatuation with India, its cultural traditions, the land, silks and spices, along with its diversity, delightfully fed our senses. This vibrant country speaks to you in ways only a queen can imagine, proclaiming her birth. That was me. Am I daydreaming?

Travel perpetually satiated us, our cups runneth over. We had an immortal love with food, glorious food, and enticing travel.

One morning, everything clicked. My passport expired. The reality of my life had to be changed. The marriage was over.

The young couple who once stood face to face and took their wedding vows, unadulterated joy emanating from my wide-open eyes, was gone. The smile I displayed could have ricocheted off the walls with the excitement of a lifetime, together with my love. Now, tears simply touch my lips.

Food was one of our many shared passions. It was salacious to engage in the flavours of life.

Now, a lost and hollow soul, utterly broken hearted, an empty shell of my former self, strong, joyous, fun-loving, and vibrant lady I used to be. Currently listless, numb, and feeling dead inside.

Simple cooking moments where gone. We once reveled in the pleasure and sensuality in each texture of eating something sexy, like strawberries dipped in silky chocolate, licking our lips. Perhaps, staring into each other's eyes, along a river café eating croissants somewhere in France…no longer enticed us.

These moments were cherished, fun recollections we experienced in Spain on our honeymoon, France, Egypt and many exotic travel places during our years together all make me long for the joy and intimacy in my life again. Coffee doesn't quite do it. I'd rather drink champagne or wine.

On our wedding day, crystal glasses sang a melody when we touched them to toast our union. The fizz reminded me of the electricity between our souls. It was the birth of a life with a partner I'd longed for and expected to live with till death do us part. We were like twin flames and mirror souls perfectly connected in unity until eternity. I called us two *peas in a pod.*

I hear myself breathing, noticing my racing heartbeat pounding on my chest, the mind clutter in my head eagerly chuntering away.

My memory evokes that feeling, a huge knot in the pit of my stomach, a physical, brutal tremor through my body and an incredible tenseness. A devastating sense of grief, sorrow, and immense sadness. I was shaking, and tears welled up in my eyes and I cuddled on my couch alone. We no longer connected.

My lethargic body, overflowing with caffeine from my little white cup with a graceful sunflower pattern. I hold the warm comforting coffee, I sip as my weepy tears struggle to be grateful for bygone times and luscious moments. Was our relationship a fraud?

What happened to our hearts and souls' synergy? I shifted from hope and joy to this state of sullenness, and my heart ached for the past. My inner being reached out hungrily for nourishment and replenishment. Anxiously, I reached deep within. Arriving at rock bottom, a misplaced and joyless woman bearing the heavy burden of melancholy, disillusionment and anger raged through me. Was this all a dream? A fantasy I formed in my mind?

Decades of being embraced in the illusion of love and adventure, it weakened, crumbled like a broken wedding cake. It was a slow and agonizing process.

We ate so much food around the world that we remembered each event with gratitude, but did we forget something? One of those delicious feasts, morsels of local sweet, savoury, juicy, sour, salty, fruity, spicy, bites brought back good memories. Did we neglect the lusciousness of cooking up new flavors in our busy lives?

Generally, tired, and tense times along with hurtful exchanges, our attitudes changed. Occasionally, stubbornness and periods of dodging and ignoring one another. How do two souls move apart to hurt one another. None of it made sense. Those bittersweet days turned into weeks, and weeks to months.

After a long, somber decade, my spark and light all burned out. Not one to cry over spilled milk.... but constantly walking on egg-shells, the marriage became sour, and had a distasteful, unsavoury taste. The spice and sweetness were gone. I was not thriving and merely surviving in a bad dream.

All the flames become lifeless ashes. Our sparks will invariably fade and die out. One day, it's our final curtain. That's the dance of life, later certainly death. Our parting saddens me to my inner core.

My 60th birthday celebration came and passed with fervent emotions of great anguish for the past, and fear for the future. We have experienced a world pandemic. I'm still here, still standing, breathing, hearing, and sensing my heartbeat. This was my wake-up hour, my catalyst for change, perhaps for others I surmised, as well.

Those years were good and exceedingly kind to us. We worked very hard, and we played the dance of life oh so well. Every adventure maintains a special place inside my heart. Did we tire of it? I wonder, and why that might be? My restless thoughts are random, and a little nonchalant today. Asking myself out loud, although I am alone, did we grow too fast? Did we ignore the spice of life?

Did we grow apart or ignore how to nurture our souls and feed each other?

I don't have all those answers. I never will. I think about it from time to time, just silent moments, and meager thoughts. It is all irrelevant now.

Egypt charmed me. Many visits… the mystery and intrigue coiled around my affections, like a cobra, the deadliest of them all. It grew like a catalyst for further adventures, but perhaps the real mystery is how it brought me to this day. I recognize now the seductress was all pretense and, in my bewilderment, blaming myself for all the things that went wrong, I discovered me.

Luxor, the most important city of ancient Egypt and the capital where the most kings lived like Tutankhamun and Ramses. It appears I'm attracted to kings; do you say? I stand before the colossal ancient columns, lined with hieroglyphics, imagining I've stood here before. Perhaps, the soul remembers and is waking me up to something. Is it why I was called back so many times? To find something I was missing?

I'm on the East Bank of the Nile, looking up at Ramesses II towering above me, pinching myself. Are we really here? A young Egyptian boy with big brown eyes, smiles and hands me a sweet red rose. I felt special. The party in the evening was magical and I took on the persona of Cleopatra with the complete veil elegant outfit. We literally 'floated' down the Nile. I could feel and imagine the spirits of lost souls around me. Not once imagining I too would be a lost soul, living in my skin, breathing but not alive in spirit.

Transported instantaneously, I remembered something from another ancient civilization. A thirst for knowledge flooded my cells. Was this my calling, to find my purpose? Did my soul reach out to connect me to something I lost?

The Egyptians believed an individual's life on earth was considered only one part of an eternal journey. The cravings I indulged in travel and exotic foods, are they really memories? They believe the soul is not one character, but a composite of different ones, each of which had its own role to play in the journey of life and the afterlife. Quite intriguing, isn't it? Considering I roam this earth seeking to find myself, this could have been a divinely guided marriage to self-discovery.

The emotional connection with Egypt most definitely enticed me and was showing me the illusion of my own life and marriage. Like a magical power, "heka," (an Egyptian term) something came over me to face the sad truths. This too, is part of the healing journey to discover one's purpose.

I have concluded our chapter, so I can be free to roam, cook, and eat around the world. Just be me, authentic me. I have found my voice and inner strength, not the old Linzi, but a new Linzi. I'm empowered, in control, and I couldn't have it any other way. This time, I am creating new dreams to come true for me.

I know now with wonderful hindsight; I neglected my own needs too many times. I was afraid and anxious for a long time. It weighed heavily on my soul. I have taken the time to soul search, heal and love myself. I'm not healed but restored or re-set. I am on a learning journey of self-discovery.

I owe it to myself to turn the page, launch a new chapter, and start a new journey. I'm open-minded. I don't know where, how, or why. I am listening to my heart and soul, paying attention to their beat and vibe.

Fresh beginnings and different endings are what I am ready for. I'm breathing and blessed. I'm going to seize every moment, every day, feel every breath of myself. I have reclaimed belief in myself and found my inner strength and freedom. I feel fortunate and optimistic about my future life and lust after joy and peace. This is what I deserve.

Yes, listening to my own needs, my heartbeat, my soul rhythm. Grateful for each breath, each glorious day, always moving forward and onwards, healing and growing. I am accepting my purpose and I'm not afraid anymore. I am no longer looking backwards. Excited, alone and so much to do. See, cook, and eat all over this planet. I am alive and could not be happier.

A bittersweet symphony, my sweet and sour story.

My soul journey begins.

Stories evoke emotions, memories and insights.
As you connect with each story you may enjoy a place
for notes, healing insights and aha moments.

Writing is powerful. Just like each author expressed
to me; writing their stories helped them heal.

I hope these pages provoke a poem perhaps,
a desire to transform your life
or merely a place to doodle your thoughts.

Write from your heart and soul,

Gloria

Bonnie Bonadeo

Bonnie has helped small business professionals as a Speaker, Brand Marketing, Mindset Coach, and Consultant for over 30 years. She believes that developing a digital presence with in-real-life (IRL) connections builds a brand as values-driven and unique.

As a licensed Cosmetologist, StoryBrand Trained Guide, Emotional Intelligent Coach, Certified NLP, TimeLine Therapy, Hypnotherapist Coach, and Trainer, her focus is guiding business owners to uncover their personal and professional brands. But, more importantly, how you promote that brand to gain loyal clients, a profitable business, and lead the life you love.

Bonnie has graced the cover of Salon Industry publications, has been mentioned in O Magazine and business journals, is a 5x International best-selling author, the founder of Brand Me Marketing & Branding Agency, host of SOS Small Business Success Podcast, SOS Salon Coaching while also working with her husband as the Marketing Director for Intrigue Salon in Atlanta, GA. In her spare time, she loves making cupcakes under her pseudo name @batshit_Bonnies_Treats

BonnieBonadeo.com FB-IG@bonniebonadeo
bonnie@bonniebonadeo.com

CHAPTER TWO

One Day, Two Loves

BONNIE BONADEO

Mom normally answers her phone or responds to my calls as soon as possible. But not this time. I glanced at the clock; the time, 2:35 pm. My heart ached with a void I could never fill as I stood before the Pet Mortuary. My sweet Lille held tightly in my arms; I thought I would never play with her again as more tears rolled down my face.

As we entered through the double doors and were greeted with a soft smile and hello from a young man, he inquired if this was Lille. He accompanied us to the chapel room to lay her down. The room smelled like fragrant flowers.

I remember my boy naming her beautiful Lille when we brought home a puppy. But he wanted to spell it differently, complicating the uncomplicated. I lean over and hold her tight as I repeat, I am so sorry; I am so sorry through every sniffle and remaining stead-fast. As I recalled the last few hours, I whispered "I hope I was a good mom to you."

Lille woke me up in the middle of the night to go potty with the tender kiss of her tongue on my cheek. Feeling exhausted, and somewhat aggravated after waking me the third time, her behavior appeared strange tonight. I noticed an odd separation from my sweet Lille, whom I adored for over fourteen years. She wandered around the kitchen while her little paws pitter pattered as expected on the wood floor. An immediate urge overcame me to rest on the floor with her and give her more mommy kisses while I whispered, "Mommy isn't mad at you," cuddling her in my lap.

My fiancé and I decided an appointment to the vet was in order and collected our belongings and hopped in the car. Ultimately, arriving at the emergency vet, I knew something was terribly wrong. Within 5 minutes of arriving, she moved into a critical state when they tried to resuscitate her. So, I requested them to stop; she needed to be at peace and not meant to return to me now. I regret not giving her more hugs and kisses as I watched her lying lifeless. Still in shock, everything happened too fast. Why did I look at my watch? 'Timing' means something?

Jeff, my fiancé, appeared distraught; although we were fortunate to love her for 14 years. Lille, my protector, cherished Jeff just the same; he, her food provider, sneaking her treats all the time. He loved her so much. We enjoy our happy little family now that my son has graduated from college and his life out west.

Both of us, uncontrollably weeping and in shock, embracing each other as so many thoughts ran through our own brains. Jeff still managed, in his grief, to locate a pet mortuary nearby. As I panicked, I could not leave her there in the cold room, filled with sadness, even with the kind vet staff. He expressed no; we are taking her somewhere else. They wrapped her in the old towel and escorted us out the rear door as I held her lifeless body tight and close to my heart.

Honestly, I don't recall many details, pacing around like a zombie, making plans for the cremation of my little buddy. Everything happened fast, decisions made, questions answered.

What about this one? I inquired. I didn't even ask his name. I pointed to a small brass container with paw prints. Being overcome with making this decision, was an understatement, as I wondered how my 7.5 lb. chihuahua ashes would fit in this urn. He stated "Yes, it's the right size," and asked if I wanted it engraved. Yes, as I thought about this finality in disbelief, should it be Little Lille, Sweet Lille, Lille Rose, or just Lille? She had so many nicknames, Lille alone felt incomplete.

After pointing to the brass urn, we headed back into the chapel to see her one last time. The kind young man approached me and asked if I wished to include her paw print. I responded yes, of course, in a soft voice while I thought to myself, please don't suggest anything else because I am going to say yes in my moment of vulnerability to everything.

We expressed our last goodbyes as Jeff and I held each other close, wondering how this happened so quickly. Why did this happen? What was wrong? Everything appeared fine yesterday; how did I not see this coming?

Looking back, knowing this was the last moment, I tried to contain my unbearable grief. Approaching the front reception, where all this emotion speedily converted into a paid transaction, we settled the bill. Jeff double-checked Lille's spelling once last time.

My phone began vibrating in my purse; my initial thought, it's mom. I must speak to her; after my eight tries earlier, I sent her a text, "Lille died, please call me." It would not have been easy to read. Digging through my purse to learn who called, it was not my mom but an Arizona cell number I didn't recognize, and I let it go. No one could be more significant than my mom at that moment, as she would provide the support desired more than anyone.

As we walked out empty-handed, confused, and troubled, the beep of a voicemail came through as we buckled up to head home, a home that would never be the same. I removed my phone and began reading the voicemail. I am so grateful for the technology of viewing a voicemail vs. listening to it. My mother's pool lady requested I call her back immediately.

If my heart had not already sunk to its lowest point, this moment of terror would settle it to the depths of despair; why would my mom's pool lady call me?

Calling her back with urgency when she spoke, "Are you sitting down?" Confused by these words, and yelling out "What happened to mom?" She shared she showed up to clean the pool and found my mom on the patio unconscious. She called 911, and they were on their way. As I heard sirens in the background, I begged her to stay on the phone with me.

Was she alive? My panicked voice quivered, asking.

"Yes, she is breathing, but can't wake up and she is pretty banged up." I couldn't even comprehend or visualize mom in this condition.

The shift from mourning my dog for less than 30 minutes quickly scrambled to find flights to fly home to Arizona and be with my mother. Once there and within 24 hours, all the doctors had assessed her; she had a catastrophic hemorrhagic stroke and would never wake up. Numb for the entire day, I stood there staring like I was suspended in a dream.

Selfishly reflecting how could I lose my dog and my mother on the same day. In unpredictable tragic circumstances, 1800 miles apart. Had someone placed a curse on me? Who would be so evil? I reflected speedily, my shock, only subsequently to be followed by denial and refusal not to accept any of it.

My grief plunged into automatic mode, planning and preparing for her, simply to find myself in another mortuary, choosing another urn to place my mother's ashes in and thinking death does not become me.

Being the youngest of three girls, along with my younger brother, who passed away at 22, my mother and I had a unique and intimate relationship. I admired her complete commitment to the family and lovingly creating a home. She had a strong stance about herself that would easily be underestimated and always made you feel important. My mom admired me for being intelligent and independent, traits I questioned for myself many times. As I made mistakes throughout life like most of us do, there was never any judgment from my mother, just love and support.

As the day ended, we went back to the house we all grew up in. This intense awareness of her presence and everything around me came to life. All the things in the house that meant something to her seemed to be humming to me in some heavenly song.

Even as the sorrow kicked in because I was unable to share the loss of my dog with my mother and losing my mother with my dog, there is some level of solace that they are together. Did Lille choose her time so I could be with my mother? Did Lille sense my mother had fallen and needed to greet her? Had they shared a secret I would never have been prepared for?

There is a saying when we pass, whether person or animal, they receive their wings… maybe so. Death, the grieving process, and learning how to live without our loved ones can force us into a cocoon, and when we eventually heal, we can break through the cocoon and fly again with our delicate but borrowed wings.

That is, until the inevitable, and we get our final wings.

I am not crying now, but I know I will be. I am not OK now, but I know I will be.

Finding peace after losing a loved one seems complicated but reflecting on the memories with my mom and my dog will ignite the healing, honoring them by sharing stories and saying their names out loud with compassion and conviction and fighting through the pain. Flutter and fly, butterfly…

In the loving memory of my mother, Doris.

In the memory of my dog, Lille.

"Just when the caterpillar thought the world was over, it became a butterfly."

All of me
GLORIA COPPOLA

The anger soared and the tears bottled up

The tightness in my chest told me I needed to escape

So, I called for help.

I thank God you were there for me

I trusted you – I'm not sure why

You helped me reach a place inside.

The emotions began to flare, you encouraged me to cry

Never once did you judge me

I felt pain, sadness, and loneliness

We laughed and cried…together

You see this was the first time I allowed someone
to see all of me.

Rodine Isfeld

Rodine Isfeld 'accidentally' discovered her talent for painting over 20 years ago and is now an award winning, internationally published artist. She uses her intuition and experience to create gorgeous artwork and her signature pieces capture the mystery and majesty of the Northern Lights.

She relishes her solo time in the studio, but as an art and English teacher, she also loves sharing her excitement for creativity and writing with her students. She is passionate about inspiring her students to see themselves as powerful and capable and designs projects that encourage genuine learning.

When she is not creating magic and messes in her studio, you will find her avoiding housework by puttering with biz work or enjoying time with her grandsons. She is also a lover of bonfires, plaid shirts and coffee!

Most of all, she is a heart-centered soul who believes in love and the healing power of art.

Facebook: Rodine Isfeld Designs
Instagram: Rodine Isfeld Designs
Website: rodineisfeld.com

CHAPTER THREE

Fear and the Art of Living

RODINE ISFELD

The sunlight cast its pale light on the treetops and the early blush of color began to wake up the world when he approached. His hands were loosely relaxing inside his pants pockets as his right foot settled firmly on the deck. He raised the rest of his body and swung his left foot to match its partner. For a figure so remarkably substantial, he proceeded with ease and drifted toward me.

"Good Morning, Fear. Joining me for coffee?"

With no threat in his eyes, but a look of warmth and, perhaps, a bit of mischief, I raised my cup to greet him hello. He proceeded towards me and lowered himself onto the cushion. With his full weight coaxing a dent from the foam underneath him, and the pressure from his leg right against mine, he nudged my shoulder, giving me a startle. He took longer to shift his body back into his own space as I wondered what he was here for today.

When Fear initially took up residence, I didn't pay attention to his presence. As insignificant as the snippets I heard at work about a new virus, he darted around me. In his infancy, much like a shadow that you notice outside of the corner of your eye. Barely perceptible, and so fleeting, it passed as nothing more than imagination. I wasn't concerned and my faith was always stronger than fear.

Like all infants, his environment affected his growth, and he spiraled into a toddler-sized, black ball with thin arms and legs who clung like a child, unwilling to let go of his mother. "What was I feeding him?" He accompanied me everywhere, clinging and climbing and jabbering all the time, pointing out potential dangers and making certain nothing harmed me. Often, I would say "Can you please go away. I have no time for fear today."

To prepare for the day, he picked up items off his shelf in a rush and crammed his backpack full of everything he assumed that would provide protection: awareness, caution, hesitancy, hyper-vigilancy... and he jammed them all down with a brick of paranoia before he zipped it up. He marginally lifted the weight of it all. "How did I allow him to take control of my life?" I questioned.

One morning, as I observed and listened to his incoherent stream of garbled sounds, something in my heart cracked open with realization. He didn't require my criticism, anger or indifference, he needed me to love him. The more I fought him, the larger he grew. I was feeding him my negative emotions.

I squatted down on the bed, patted my hand on the mattress and invited him to come meet with me. His movements slowed, but he continued packing. He didn't trust well and became wary and skeptical of my intent.

I approached him with tenderness and compassion. Whispering, I told him "I know how scary it can be and its OK. We are going to be just fine. I promise I will take care of us." He wasn't responsible for me. I loved him so much for everything he did for me and appreciated him. He didn't have to bear that heavy backpack...

I would take over. At least I hoped I had the courage and tenacity to do so. It wasn't getting easier that's for sure.

Not trusting me, he reached for the brick of paranoia, struggling to dislodge it with his tiny hands, glanced at me questioningly, and hesitantly laid it on the bed. I smiled and nodded. He sighed and withdrew another item, raised his eyebrows, and after reassurance from me he did just fine. As his pack became lighter, he became softer. The hardness of his body became fuzzy and the dark core an impermeable pulsation with the slow steadiness of breathing.

Chattering under his breath, he shuffled his way to me, climbed up my legs and awkwardly maneuvered himself until he plopped his bottom on my lap and rested the top of his roundness on my chest, and together we exhaled.

As he sunk into me, I cradled him, nestling my face on the top of his head. Rocking him tenderly, and acknowledged him by saying, "Do you know how brave you are? You always protect me in all precarious situations. Thank you love, it means a lot to have you on my side." Love flowed between us, and his tears stopped.

Fear matured with gentleness, compared to anxiety. While Fear wanted to jangle my nerves so I would remain home in bed, Anxiety preferred to smash the shit out of everything. A nasty bastard with a cigarette hanging from his mouth and a switchblade tucked away in his boot. He preferred to throw punches and leave bruises, but one day, he went too far. I recognized Anxiety from previous situations in my life that became overwhelming.

In a classic move, he backed me against the wall. He wrapped his hands around my throat and dug his fingers into my trachea, while spitting and laughing in my face that I was going to die. "You are going to die! You will die alone!" he growled. Choking, my heart racing and tears cascading down my face, I reasoned with him until he would lose his grip. Eventually, he stepped back. Just enough to deliver a final punch to my stomach and force me to vomit.

"Stop it! You're hurting her!" Fear cried as he held my head, doing his best to make me comforting.

Anxiety scoffed. "I'm just toughening her up. She honestly believes that caring so much for her students is going to create a difference. Such a sucker. Seriously?" I held my tears and fear back as much as possible as his words were speaking truth. "You get on my nerves," murmuring through my tight lips.

"Greeting her students outside with a smile before they all protect their faces is noble. Reminding them to sanitize and stay two feet apart all day is honorable? Making certain they aren't scared, acting like everything is 'normal' for them while she is scared shitless isn't noble, it's foolish."

Gosh, he was making sense and rambled on some more. "Does she really believe that anyone would acknowledge her sacrifice if she died? She's not a 'frontline worker,' she's just a teacher."

While nonchalantly leaning against the bathroom door jam, Death calmly stated, "Oh Anxiety, you are such a drama monger. I am simply a part of life, not some monster standing by to devour her. Stop your ridiculous rants… you're exhausting." By now the voices in my head were taking over and I couldn't stop it.

As Fear cradled me, and Anxiety petulantly stepped back, I took in every feature of Death. Not an ounce of malevolence or trickery was evident. Nothing threatening in his demeanor. Not scary. He was just there. Peaceful and supportive.

I made a choice about his role in my life, and at that moment, I concluded we could be friends.

While attempting to understand him and manage the new guests who occupied my inner world, my outer–all appeared fine. But if you watched, the whitened tips of my fingers were losing their precarious grip on a cliff, and I desperately needed a footing to rest.

I needed to take a break to heal. I was terrified I would lash out at a student because, emotionally, my frustrations, pain and constant panic were so acute. My brain was in full-on survival mode and unable to tell the difference between real or perceived as a threat. I felt dangerous to myself.

The thought I could unintentionally hurt a student made my heart so sad and added a thick, gummy layer of guilt. The PTSD, like a virus, grew daily as I'm certain it did for many others. Our coping mechanisms were breaking down. I'm sure I was not alone… all because of Anxiety and Fear.

I went on leave from teaching. I started to hear whispers. They would pop up during the day and tickle my ears or tease my consciousness, and then flit away, just like a tune you can't quite recall. Within a week, those whispers shifted from being little nudges from the outside to a stirring so deep I couldn't ignore it.

I felt untethered. I didn't call friends. I ceased painting. People rarely came to visit, and I seldom went to visit anyone. I became isolated in my house. I felt disconnected, not only from the people I loved and everything I believed defined me and gave me purpose, but from my source of love, God. The Universe. No amount of prayer or meditation or yoga or visualization seemed to ease the emptiness, and I had become numb.

A nothing.

In my state of nothingness, the silence and safety of my home allowed me to breathe. The violence of Anxiety abated, and the incessant chatter of Fear somewhat diminished. I heard the child-like giggles of joy that tinkled before they evaporated. They would pop up during the day and tickle my ears or tease my consciousness and later flit away. Their invitation invited me to go play with my paints. It was the first time I felt Joy since Anxiety had taken over my brain.

The ritual of art can be powerful. Joy lifted my favorite brush from the stand and placed it in my hand. I smiled as I recalled the many times when those tiny bits of bristle fluttered through the air. Sometimes they lodged themselves in the landscape of a painting. Worn and weathered, the faded white paint on the handle had chipped away. It looked like me.

My life is breaking apart. The sense of heaviness from the pressure had me reflecting upon the vibrancy of the North Lights. Divine light splashed across the heavens with such intensity. Such brilliance. Always with the offer to fill your soul with childlike wonder, Joy reminded me today how wonderful it all feels.

I gracefully ran my fingers over the tips of bristles, one by one, deliberately re-membering. The phthalo green made me sigh. The chameleon color of the sky that vibrates with power and unapologetic radiance. Joy compelled me to raise the brush to the tip of my nose, a gentle inhale of the lingering scent of oil paints and the distinct acidity of thinner. I recognized the soft stirrings of peace inside me, and Anxiety disappeared.

Scraping the blobs of oil paint, working them from rigid blobs into creamy, smeary piles of joy and the rhythmic drumbeat of the brush striking the canvas as the oil layer was applied, brought up feelings of calm that I had not known in years.

Joy wanted to slather the magnificent royal purple first. My hand pulled back with a bit of resistance. I recognized Fear had joined me. Turning my head, I spotted him perched on the top rail of the chair, feet on the seat and leaning forward with his chin resting on his knees. Not a toddler, but in that awkward stage between teen and adult, his expression, a mix of trepidation and anticipation with a hint of 'I dare you' in his eyes.

Casually turning away, I took a deep breath, held it, surrendered to Joy, and exhaled myself into the sounds and rhythms and smells to develop into the creator of my masterpiece. As I dragged my hand downward and crisscrossed my loaded brush onto the canvas, I knew Joy had granted me the grace of reconnection to the creator.

Painting Northern Lights with oils is an artistic alchemy. I added the colors on top of a black canvas. Colors that will be born as lights are mysteriously concealed, graceful, merely to be gifted life and movement with the enhancement of white. This is where I occasionally feel like I'm painting blind. The shape and movement and colors are going to be as much a surprise to me as they are when someone first looks at a finished piece.

The further Joy immersed me in my paints, the more open I became to discovering the tints and shades. They fully understood I needed the darker shades to balance out the rest of the landscape. As the ultimate creator, I was in control of how much of the dark I allowed on the canvas. I could let it dominate and overpower and turn everything into mud, or I would manage it to add depth, richness and a companion of the light. Quite a metaphor for life.

Joy's perspective shifted my view of my life and when I saw Fear, he ceased to be the child who ran the house and became a friend. I am grateful for his presence because I recognize he was never an adversary. Rather, someone who cherished me so deeply that he would carry everything to protect me. He kept me safe when I couldn't. Fear didn't represent my weaknesses but became the champion of my strengths. He never needed the job of being responsible for my life, but he voluntarily held me until I held my own.

The balance, just like the ebb and flow of dark and light; the darkness no longer overcame me during these tumultuous times. I could shine my light and bring Joy as comfort and grace flowed through me now. I was stronger. Maybe I needed a break from all of life to see the creator in new ways. Perhaps to experience my strength and to dab a sparkle and little glitter upon my masterpiece. It was my solace, my medicine of choice.

I know in my soul that art heals. Creativity begs to be allowed to play with each inner child and will unabashedly celebrate the freedom of our Divine wildness. We are free to play with curious abandon and make all kinds of concoctions. Some will be delightful and make us smile or gasp in awe. While others may turn into a series of lessons that guide us forward. It gifts us time, that moment, where we accept that what we will birth is a mystery, but we are full of wonder as we await its arrival.

Lately, when Fear joins me for coffee, he nudges me with his shoulder and asks me how I am. I tell him.

"I'm Good. I'm really good. I'd like to introduce you to Joy."

"*Art is a way of recognizing oneself.*"

–Louise Bourgeois

Dina Baker

Dina Baker is an Intuitive Vocalist, Reiki and Emotion Code Certified Practitioner.

She has been in the healing arts for over 20 years, originally starting her journey as a Licensed Massage Therapist.

Following a profound experience that expanded her connection to Creator God, the Ancestors and Angelic Realm, her voice awakened, and she became a channel for chanting divine magical sounds she refers to as sacred soul songs.

Her belief in the healing power of the voice fuels her passion for singing, using sound to re-harmonize chaotic energy and shift low vibe fears into peaceful bliss and clarity.

Dina provides a safe nurturing space where the mysteries deep within one's own heart can be unlocked for self-exploration and healing on all dimensions, including physical, mental, emotional and spiritual.

She is married to an amazing man who lovingly supports her endeavors, has a beautiful artistic daughter, and a crazy hairless dog that keeps them all laughing. She enjoys watching the sun rise, taking long walks in nature and spending countless hours looking for seashells when she gets to visit family at the beach.

www.soundbodyawakenings.com
dina@soundbodyawakenings.com

CHAPTER FOUR

Vibrations with Purpose

DINA BAKER

"Oh SHIT! I just did that. He's going to KILL me!" Tears full of mascara and slimy snot were cascading down my face.

It was a balmy and humid summer evening. The kind of weather that turns a gal's smooth hair into a pile of frizzy chaos. You know, the kind that depicts one's life. Well, at least mine. Altogether uncontrollable and frying my nerves to a crisp.

Seeking to enjoy a carefree, romantic, and delightful evening out with my friends, no doubts entered my thoughts. But, just like always, my boyfriend humiliated me and made me feel like a piece of shit. I had no sense of self and felt worthless. It was at a time when I was naïve and had no voice of my own. This was the "norm". Should I be used to it by now? Maybe, but not OK with it at all.

It was time to celebrate with my friends on the dance floor. Woo hoo! After sipping down a few Mai Tai's, I was ready to cut loose and have some fun when "Brown Eyed Girl" started playing over the speakers. It was so intense my partner motioned for me to hold his hand and brought me into the crowd. We were smiling and chuckling. Golden candlelight glimmered from fashionable centerpieces with white aromatic lilies. He was spinning me around in my alluring dress, thoroughly reveling in the moment, with beads of perspiration accumulating on our foreheads.

The DJ started fading into a song for slow dancing. My partner wrapped his firm hands around my slender waistline and drew me in tight to him. Finally! We're having a wonderful time and he's actually being nice. My arms and shoulders melted as we swayed with the rhythm. He leaned in and whispered, "Hey, you see that girl over there?"

"Which one? The one with the long blond hair?"

"Yeah."

I rolled my eyes. Here we go again. "What about her?"

"She's fucking hot and her ass looks amazing. She must work hard in the gym. You'll never look as good as she does, no matter what you do."

A fake smile rolled across my face while my heart collapsed. Instantly, I pressed my tongue to the roof of my mouth, struggling to avoid crying and the swelling in my eyes. "Not today and not here," I declared. Get a grip. He had made similar comments to me before. I never felt good enough. He knocked down my self-esteem all the time, and I allowed it by putting up with this crap.

Immediately forcing myself to take a full breath, "Dear God, just whatever transpires, please do NOT let me have a panic attack here."

As the song ended, I wiggled my way out of his arms and made a beeline for the ladies' room. My close friend was already using the rest room. She opened one of the stall doors, saw the upset expression on my face and asked, "What's wrong?" That's all it took. My shoulders shuddered as a stream of tears gushed down my face.

She swiftly clutched my hand and took me outside. "What happened?"

"Oh, the usual," I mumbled. "Another fight is inevitable if he sees me like this. Let's go sit in my car."

I plopped down into the passenger seat of my car as my friend walked around to sit in the driver's seat. Pretty ironic, because I didn't sense I was steering my life in the right direction at all. God only knows how long it had been since I had voiced my opinion on anything or listened to the promptings of my intuition.

Sitting, sobbing, I repeated what my partner had said to me. Her eyes opened wide, and jaw dropped when she blurted with a concerned tone, "What are you going to do? This has been happening for a long time. I hate seeing you like this. I want to see you happy."

"I knowww!!" bellowing out as I met no resistance. "I'm SO over it! His condescending remarks and constant drilling of my whereabouts make me sick to my stomach, and I can't stand it when he grabs my face and backs me into a wall."

My voice continued escalating as I rocked back and forth, pounding the seat with clenched fists like a toddler having a hissy fit. On the dashboard, my perfectly pedicured feet with pink polish adorned in black strappy heels started kicking. Uninterrupted and forceful.

Physically exhilarating, internally my soul was dying. With his relentless criticism, I was emotionally and spiritually lost, separated from God, out of alignment and forlorn.

Speaking up for myself was hard; I didn't feel pretty or smart enough, and weight loss was my obsession. I had dropped out of college with no money saved and the extent of my prayers were, "Please, God, help me."

As I squealed at the top of my lungs, "I just can't take it anymore!" my high-heeled foot slipped off the dash and kicked the windshield. Right before my eyes, I observed the glass shatter into pieces, just like me. Shivering in my seat, my heart fluttered with pure amazement.

Somewhat giddy from disbelief of what just took place, we both burst into wild laughter. It felt so good to cut loose, be free in my expression and let out pent-up emotions! There "she" was, my intuitive voice. I wished to savor this revelatory moment of deep self-reconnection.

When was the last time my voice connected to powerful energy? It was eons ago, at age eleven, when I got baptized in the Holy Spirit.

I recall strolling up to the velvety maroon upholstered prayer bench, the Pastor's warm hand settled on the top of my head while being surrounded by a few other praying adults. My body trembled and my tongue quivered with a deluge of energy that practically knocked me over as I started shouting ineffable messages.

My heart had always craved to fulfill God's plan for my life with meaning and purpose, but I didn't think I was good enough.

In my soul, I understood what I was yearning for: complete love and acceptance. Truthfully, I needed to love and respect MYSELF. This would fuel me with the permission to accept my voice.

Years later, I'd have my second pivotal awakening.

The day after my father's passing, with a pocket full of tissues and a grieving heart, I boarded my early morning flight headed to the enchanting island of Kauai for a Lomilomi massage training.

Our Kumu, a teacher, greeted us, placing sweetly fragranced purple orchid leis over our heads. "We'll be going to a heiau, a sacred site, to facilitate a memorial service for Dina's dad. Poli Hale is known as the place where souls shift from this plane of existence through a portal or passageway to the spiritual realm. "First," she announced, "we're going to learn about how the indigenous people used to chant."

My eyes opened wide like someone had just hailed my name for a grand winning prize. Chills crawled up the nape of my neck, like I was just reminded of something I intuitively recognized how to do, unlocking a past lifetime memory. Whoa. Somewhat stunned, I leaned back, shifting my crossed legs to take in a full sigh.

In the night's stillness, it was time to return to our retreat home. The sun was nearly set while we traveled down a rugged dirt road illuminated by the crescent moon as the warm orange sun disappeared below the horizon. The group had an unusual urge to stop, prompting Kumu to slam on the brakes. My head jolted back and forth as the tires skidded to a standstill.

After getting out of the car, we paused beside the landscape. We gazed up at the night sky, lit with a gazillion of the luminous stars we had ever witnessed. Our focus rapidly shifted to a cloud formation that was in the shape of God's hands. Love was received, feeling cherished, like it was a gesture my dad was with me. "This place really is magical."

The tranquility turned into a palpable presence, with the pause of breath between inhalation and exhalation. Kumu turned to me. "Dina, they have a message for you."

This profound silence supported me to connect to my inner voice as I heard, "This is what we do. We sing and chant to support the journey of bringing the spirit to the light. Do not be afraid. You are helping to prepare the way. There is rejoicing in their return home as we open the portal for their transmittance into the light."

Spontaneously, I moved into a focused channeling process as my body moved cathartically. It seemed like a bolt of lightning infiltrated my field and plugged me into a continuous pulsating electrical current.

Trembling from head to toe, quaking and shaking in ways that mirrored my church days of speaking in tongues, dancing in the aisles, and getting slain in the spirit. A mighty energy began rising from my belly that penetrated my chest and throat as I belted out strange sounds and tones that morphed into an unfamiliar language. In my euphoria, I had no inhibitions.

A group of loving women who were holding space for me enveloped the moment. They had energetically formed a cocooned field of protection around me while I was quite engaged in divine consciousness. On the outside, I didn't notice what they were witnessing, but I felt their presence of support to be myself without judgment. These women were standing strong with me.

The evolution of my gift used songs that traversed across a decade. Channeling transformed from feeling like I was riding a wild bull to floating on ocean waves. I joyfully traded out racy heart palpitations, jitters in my belly and trembling arms and hands for softer heart flutters, relaxed breaths, and a steady melodic resonance.

During morning meditations, my perceptive voice would perk up like a personal cheerleader. "I give you permission to BE you! You must wholeheartedly trust your own inclinations and, above all, have faith and don't give up."

"But I don't want to sound crazy."

"There's no time for that. It takes guts to be comfortable in your own skin. No matter how vulnerable or uncomfortable, allow yourself to be heard."

My angels would chime in, "We're always here upholding you. Trust your connection to God, your Source. Believe in yourself. You can do it. We didn't bring you this far to drop you in the middle of nowhere."

Sometimes the expression of my voice and who I am is still a struggle, but the more I listen and allow the flow of intuitive promptings, the easier it has become, like second nature.

I've grown fond of experiences where I have appeared safe expressing my voice with others who gratefully accept the songs and messages. A shiver rushes down my spine when I hold the presence of a loved one that has crossed over. My scalp tingles as angels and spirit beings enter space. When the sounds rise from the depths of my heart, my soul reiterates "All I want to do is to be on a stage with a microphone and sing!"

I had a discussion with a trusted friend. "All I crave to do is sing! I desire to record these melodic vocals."

"You definitely need to do that. Your voice is amazing, and I'm constantly surprised by what it does for me. It's like you're opening my third eye. The feeling is like being cradled in my mother's arms, which is such a blessing since she's passed from this life."

We paused and took a deep breath as she became teary-eyed.

"I realize you call yourself a vocal mystic, so I think it'd be highly fitting if you called yourself Vocal Mystic Mama."

Giggling simultaneously, I allowed the name to filter into my field. At that moment, I opened permission to fully embrace the new me that was emerging.

"Yes! Vocal Mystic Mama is exactly who I am!"

"And the day came when the risk to remain tight in a bud was more painful than the risk it took to blossom."

–Anais Nin

Lauren Raguzin
CHANGE MANAGEMENT AND COMMUNICATIONS

Lauren Raguzin has loved writing since she was ten years old. She started her career as a secretary in a large advertising agency and has been in communications for 20 years. She has an entrepreneurial mindset but has spent most of her career working for corporate companies.

While a writer by trade, her life-long dream was to be published in a book one day.

She loves teaching and mentoring others; she has taught undergraduate and graduate school for the last 15 years, and her greatest joy is helping others find their passion, especially in communications.

Lauren is married and lives in Clayton, NC, with her loving husband, John Raguzin, a two-time cancer survivor, her soulmate and best friend, and her two fur babies, Cinnamon and Skippy, Cavalier King Charles spaniels. In her free time, she loves cooking and creating videos for her Pampered Chef Healthy Cooking Facebook page, www.facebook.com/healthylauren/.

Lauren is a lifelong learner and risk taker, not afraid of change, and she embraces it; she credits all she has achieved in her life only through God's grace. She cherishes her spiritual journey and relationship with God the most.

To connect with Lauren, reach out to her via email: lraguzin123@gmail; she loves connecting with new people on LinkedIn, and she is the only Lauren Raguzin (https://www.linkedin.com/in/laurenraguzin/) or Facebook - @healthylauren

CHAPTER FIVE

The Day God Came to my Pity Party

LAUREN RAGUZIN

It was Day 372, another day of darkness and no light, but it wasn't physically dark, the bright sun glistened through my bedroom window, and Christmas was two weeks away, my favorite time of the year. You would think Grinch lived with me; not one decoration adorned any room in my house, no tree or nativity scene.

I opened my eyes, I had to wipe away the crust on my moist eyelashes and pry them open. 2 hours prior, I awoke at 4:00 a.m. and started crying, no trigger, a frequent occurrence for me. I knew this all too well. My routine was to silence my tears with the pillow over my face. Then my husband wouldn't hear me sob or listen to me sniffling.

Life isn't always rosy, and for me, it's been a hard life. The sudden loss of my father at 19, the painful loss of my best friend, and watching her die an agonizing death. My husband scared me to death when he was diagnosed with cancer after kicking cancer's butt 20 years ago. Brutal stuff, but I got through it.

God was with me every step of the way. I always felt his presence and love, but now nothing. I was alone, scared. Didn't feel his presence, the most heart wrenching of all, abandoned. Why? My closeness with God disappeared.

It's hard to admit you are a control freak, but it's true. I have always had a hand in every aspect of my life, planning everything meticulously, so I'm never surprised or blindsided.

The day came when I was no longer needed, yes, replaceable. In my case, a layoff, a devastating experience, the first in my career. Dreaded emotions and voices in my head told me I was a loser. How ashamed and embarrassed, my posture was depressing. My heart sank when I was told on the phone. Imagine a 30-story building crashing down on top of me and no one around to dig me out, quite frightening indeed.

I kept hearing in my head; "YOU failed, Lauren." My ego was irreparably damaged. "You are an utter and complete failure." I struggled to keep my voice from quaking during this fateful phone call, days after returning from a Florida getaway for my birthday, after being told to take a break. Few knew how scared and alone this all was for me, not even my husband. I'm too strong, you know, to show my vulnerability.

I've always been the one who decided to leave a job; this time, fate stepped in, and it was a crushing blow. How dare they not see my value and worth? "Lauren, you are amazing. What would we do without you?" I was told only weeks ago. What happened?

When you leave a job (there is control), you can prepare for the transition and feel emotions, but you call the shots because you made the decision. But when you are laid off and blindsided, it's a gut-wrenching blow to your gut and ego. I felt worthless. I realized my career defined my self-worth.

This pain was foreign to me. What is wrong with me? Why wasn't I good enough? Wow, a severe loss of my dignity. Nothing made me happy or excited. Even taking a shower was overwhelming to me. I couldn't snap out of it, no matter how hard I tried.

Many close to me always say, "Lauren, you are the strongest person I know." It's a catch-22 for me. I like that people think I'm strong, but it's hard to live up to it every day. Whenever someone said that to me, I wanted to scream, "No, I'm not! It's too much. I'm weak, lost, and need help!" but I never said anything. So how could I dispel the strong image everyone had of me?

Now it was my time to ask for help. Gulp. The fear of rejection was stifling, and I couldn't allow myself to be disappointed. What if no one helps me?

Asking others for help is probably the hardest thing I struggle with daily. I find it very difficult to ask others for help, and I know why. That horrid word we hide from, rejection. This pattern has continued throughout my adult life. If I don't ask someone for help, I can't and won't be disappointed. I have conditioned myself and built such a wall. I'm the helper, and I like it that way. I'm the one everyone comes to for advice and help. It makes me feel good.

Desperate times were creeping up, and I was constantly dipping into my investment portfolio. I bit the bullet. It was so hard, but I reached out to many past peers throughout my career, people I regarded as good "work" friends, and colleagues who "said" they respected me. Crickets, it was deafening, unreturned calls, ignored emails, and yes, some unfriended and disconnected from me on professional networks.

Disappointed and rejected, this only made me feel more embarrassed and ashamed. Again, the voice in my head, "Lauren, don't let anyone know how weak and scared you are. If you do, you will only be disappointed." I fell into a more profound depression.

Sleep became my new best friend; with the soft blankets tightly wrapped around my body. It was comfortable, safe, and warm. Sleep was a wonderful escape and a safe hiding place from everyone, everything, but mostly me.

The same week when I did reach out, my husband said, "Honey, you must snap out of this. You control your mindset. We will be OK. Where is your faith?"

While these were all good questions, how could he be so cruel? How dare he say to me, "Where is your faith?"

Why couldn't he see how broken I was? Didn't he love or care about me? Well, it angered me even more. I had faith in God, but the financial stress was crushing me. I saw no way out. If this continues, we will have to sell our house. How would we ever afford another with no savings and no job?

And how dare he question my faith? I prayed every day alone, only to feel completely abandoned by God. Where was God when I needed help? I stopped going to church. It was not a place I wanted to go. I was always tired, had no energy, and was a shell of my former self. In my head, repeating the dreaded question, "Have you found a job yet?" I would nod politely while my insides were screaming, "No, please help me!"

I prayed and talked to God daily, but I didn't know where to look, empty inside and abandoned. So why wasn't he helping me?

There was a big hole in my heart. I have always sensed God's presence before, but not now. Was he mad at me for not going to church? Was he angry about my thoughts of going to sleep and not waking up? Was he disappointed I wasn't helping people anymore?

Thoughts of mounting financial debt consumed me. How will I support us? When I married John, I always knew I would need to support us, and it never bothered me because I found my soul mate, best friend, and the love of my life. But now I was so alone. What will happen to us if I don't find a job?

Why wasn't I grateful for being alive? Why wasn't I thankful for having a roof over my head? Why, Why, Why?

Little things in life have always brought me the greatest happiness. My life was now a black hole, like a scene in a movie I was being buried alive. Nothing made me happy, no joy, laughter was hard. Even though my husband is hilarious, I couldn't laugh or smile.

I remember frequently thinking, what if I died in my sleep? At least John would be taken care of with my pension and Social Security. But mostly, I thought I would escape the pain of waking up each day.

My days and nights were lying lifeless in bed, like a rotted sack of potatoes. I would often lock the door so if my husband came into the room, he wouldn't see me crying and scold me for feeling sorry for myself. When crying subsided, playing mindless games on my phone worked until my eyes got heavy so I could sleep and not think about anything or anyone.

Why couldn't I escape this abyss of darkness? Why wasn't I asking anyone for help? But I was. I prayed and talked to God...but deafening silence.

I only spoke to my mother regularly because I didn't want her to worry or know I was truly depressed I was. I would keep our conversations superficial and short. That's what was manageable before the tears well up in my eyes, and then my voice would quake, muting myself worked so she couldn't hear my mini bursts of sobbing.

Every day I would wake up and say to myself, "OK, Lauren, today is the day you snap out of this. Today is the day you go for a walk. Today you feel God's presence." Well, the days blurred into weeks and months.

Then it finally happened. Day 373 arrived when I woke up with no crusted eyelashes. I woke up refreshed and remembered the day as if it was yesterday…December 16, 2019. God was HERE! Waking up happy, how is this possible? I woke up from a coma and a surge ran through me to conquer the world.

There he was, like a fire in my soul, and a bright light switched in my head. God's presence was back. He came to my pity party! "Yes," I said it out loud, the pathetic pity party I created. God was the last to arrive with the best gift of all, getting my joy and life back.

What a feeling to not dread the start of my day but be happy, to be alive as the morning sunlight greeted me and my eyes opened without me prying them open.

And all one week before Jesus' birthday, hmmm, coincidence, definitely not. This was the start of his plan for me. I still had no prospect for a job, but I was happy again and no longer afraid or scared. God was beside me!

The next morning, I got up and took my dog for a long walk, the first in 372 days. I created an online portfolio of all my work. I didn't have one, so you are probably sitting here thinking, so why did you make an online portfolio. Big deal. Well it was a big deal for me. Not only was God's presence back, but my confidence in me was also back.

Damn, I realized, Lauren, you are incredibly talented. I didn't fail, they didn't appreciate what they had in me, and God had a bigger and better plan for me.

God coming to my pity party made me realize my focus was on poor little me and convincing myself that living in an abysmal black hole was my fate.

There is no other explanation. You don't wake up one day after 372 days of depression and are ready to take on the world.

Things started falling into place. I found a part-time job and started teaching again, with minimal pay, driving 100 miles three times a week. I was happy, joyfully happy. Shortly after the teaching gig ended, a recruiter called, and I landed a job.

The most beautiful thing was how the Holy Spirit was flowing. Every morning I got up, prayed, was directed to a song, and wrote prayers which I posted on Facebook. I would marvel at how the songs would find me and the words in my blessings, not my own. I have these prayers printed in a book in my office, and when I say them, I realize God was healing me and helping me heal others with my words.

Now, three years later, I'm the happiest I have ever been. I still struggle with asking others for help. These are baby steps for me, but this experience gave me great empathy for others. Now, I try and help strangers struggling with job loss. I get it.

As I look back, I'm thankful for the experience. The biggest lesson in all this is I realized I needed to change my behavior and make God a focus of my life every day...humans can and will disappoint us but when we trust, thank, and praise God, his love is unconditional, and God never disappoints.

And yes, asking for help is still a struggle, but baby steps. We need to ask for help; if we don't, we rob others of joy.

"When a deep injury
is done to us, we never heal
until we forgive."

—Nelson Mandela

Paolina Jacobi

Paolina Jacobi is an inquisitive spirit who loves learning and connecting with others. Her love for languages and cultures surfaced as a child and continued while studying Organizational Communications and romance languages at the University of Wisconsin-Milwaukee. Born in Milwaukee to parents who met in Italy, an American father and Italian mother.

Paolina began her career as a bilingual grief, and reframing life coach after leaving her lucrative job in Wall Street to care-give for her mother overseas in Italy. A selfless task that lasted almost eight years. After her mother's passing, many unresolved emotions surfaced during the grieving process. To name a few, loss of identity, guilt, shame along with several stages of pre-grieving, (moments of advanced mourning as the person declines. She sought out therapy and coaching and saw how it helped her to heal.

Paolina became a certified health and life coach whose mission is to not let women walk the deep dark path of caregiving or grief alone, and to help these women heal their hurting hearts by learning to live, love, and laugh again by Evolving with Love.

https://NewHorizons-Coaching.com
Paolina@newhorizons-coaching.com
Facebook Paolina Jacobi + New Horizons-Coaching
You Tube Paolina Jacobi
Instagram Paolina Jacobi
Linked In New Horizons Coaching Paolina Jacobi

CHAPTER SIX

Per Amore! For Love!

PAOLINA JACOBI

The moment of truth arrived when the chief physician took me aside and delivered the cold, hardened facts. A message so gray just as the day began, no one wishes to learn. He stated, "Every day is a gift" and my mom could die at any minute. "Let her have whatever she desires, including cigarettes or a stiff drink."

I had to digest this and analyze it. It's what I do even in my career. It's natural for me to ask questions and consider resolutions in situations. We don't realize the magnitude of something we have been bearing until it has been removed. It did not prepare me for my mother to age, to be ill, and to care for her.

Many thoughts penetrated my mind from what started as always, a joyous, loving morning routine filled with singing and smiles, mom's shower, to witnessing what presented to be an epileptic convulsion. It came suddenly after I told her I would not leave my high-profile job on Wall Street to bring her to Italy.

Was this another one of her temper tantrums and shrewd ploys for attention to get what she demanded? She collapsed, convulsing in my arms. How I remain calm to lay her down, I'll never know.

Like an atomic explosive, my body exploded outwardly. In shock, yelling hysterically, totally incapacitated and racing through the house yelling, help her, cover her, call the ambulance someone.

Every sense in my being went numb, other than cry and run. It mimicked being so drunk where you can't recall anything. I needed to be slapped. I wondered if the new trial medicine she took gave her an adverse reaction or my words. I broke a promise, and a promise is a debt! That same commitment kept her alive with hope for the past year.

I must be strong. My job now consisted of protecting and communicating for her. When we age, our long-term memory works better than our short-term. Mom reverted to her native language, Italian. The ambulance ride and time to the emergency room were so horrifying, watching mom scream over and over while vomiting into an oxygen mask. I wasn't ready for this. I desired to understand what my mother communicated. I realized she felt sad living in America. As a widow, it added to her discontent.

I am an empath. I could sense the seriousness of what it meant to her, to go home. Was she fighting for her sovereignty and last chance at living? Did she know spiritually her death was inevitable?

I was born an extremely sensitive being. I regularly felt other people's suffering and pain. I found it harder to discern with those closest to me. An empath chooses to connect with others in distress. It was time to tap into the Universe. Confused about how to deal with this from the emotional level, I engaged my task master. A discussion with God was in order, so I could accomplish this purpose. "Be open to new experiences, places, and faces. It will be a chance for you to learn more."

As the divine whispered to me, sharing the benefits of going, I felt a joy in saying YES. God said, "Everything will be taken care of. You will receive many gifts and blessings." Thoughts went racing through my mind. I could find out more about my 'italianita' what it is to be Italian and Bolognese. I could study the history, the language, more about my ancestors, my culture, my mother, along with some energetic ancestral healing. Perhaps I could identify who I truly am and where I belong.

Growing up ethnically like the movie, "My Big Fat Greek Wedding," one is laughed at school, eating ethnic meals, while others eat sandwiches. Being first generation on one side of the pond made it tough for me. I had no sense of self. Whether in America or Italy, a misfit who doesn't belong or not good enough continued to be a theme in my life. I seldom felt the love I desired.

It was then God placed me face-to-face with **Fago**. *A word/emotion that comes from the Caroline Islands. A woven emotion of love, compassion, and sadness all in one. It's the empathy/pity we feel for our cherished ones, and it propels us to tend to them while realizing we will lose them.*

A surge of warmth and messages came to me: *My last act of Love!* I'll show her how good I can be. I'll give the gift of life and fulfill my mother's wishes! She went through so much during WWII, being in America, and she sacrificed a lot for us.

Feeling inadequate ran through my life, relationships, and career. I felt fake and accepting maternal caregiving would be my breakout of jail free card. Before helping mom, I watched the sun rise while sipping my coffee. I made my decision. With my heart pounding profusely, I anxiously picked up the phone. Battling internally because everything I achieved, the things I challenged myself to do, were about to drift away. I wasn't clear what my life would encompass, and this call frightened me.

"Hello Boss," my voice faint and shaky, unlike my usual boisterous personality, I continued. "The Family care time is almost up, and you need an answer. Because of the health needs of mom, I'm not coming back." As an outstanding leader, my boss provided options and alternatives to make it work. A win/win for both. After all, I demonstrated myself by sustaining seven high-profile mergers and received many promotions. He tried other means, but my inner guide declared 'choose love and give life.' I wept, after all I had been with the company for over 25 years. I offered to be available to support a smooth transition.

The days continued; I gave away almost all my belongings. One has to let go to let in. Next, I purchased our tickets since Italy became essential to sustaining her. She always lit up reminiscing about her country. We took off with two suitcases per person and embarked on our new way of life. The vibrancy she emanated on the airplane, like another person. I made the correct choice.

Initially, things went smoothly, even though we were without a car. My everyday duties entailed wearing many hats and multi-tasking. My opportunity to demonstrate my love arrived. Mom's doctor visited. He knew what my mother endured: PTSD, cancer survivor, a widow, and subsequently battered by her partner.

He congratulated me, declaring most individuals at 80 remain the same or digress. Mom improved remarkably. It's because, with fun and laughter, I involved her in tasks to demonstrate she was healthy and not infirm. We traveled out every day and developed a relationship we never knew.

She always told me we were best friends, but never showed it to me. Often, I wasn't good enough, I felt worthless. I didn't deny my mother anything but denied myself everything. Compassion would be my approach, but don't get me wrong, I had my occasions of irritation and anger, sporadically raged. I felt awful about this. However, I'm human.

Life at all costs, my motto I lived by. I discovered the importance of getting out of the house and treating her in a favorable, gracious way.

This is when I learned the wind is also an energetic healer while on the beach one day. I called it 'a wind bath.' We would both respond in a better mood, like getting a shower. In cooler or inclement weather times, I would drive my mom around. One time, too drained to respond no, I fell asleep driving. By the grace of God we survived, including most of the car. The things we do for love.

The hardest pills to swallow were role reversals, along with feeling powerless during certain situations. As mom deteriorated, more situations unfolded. There is a painful process of obtaining and maintaining health and peace and not knowing what to expect. Navigating these new waters was lonely. I had no outlet for me nor breaks to communicate my fears and struggles.

As each day passed, I realized there were more days behind than ahead. Not knowing how much time we had left; I did everything in my power to give her hope and a sense of normalcy.

To give her a sense of Love and hope, I allowed her to have a boyfriend in the house for two and a half months. It worked well for her; I saw her health and demeanor improve. She enjoyed being a seductress, goddess type. But the two octogenarians were overwhelming. I could barely tend to my mom and my duties. The boyfriend, demanding and abusive, provided no support. A tough decision would be made if he went one step too far. While the boyfriend lived at the house, we were both dying. We both needed help. She experienced three heart attacks in one day. Mom survived with only 40% of the heart and it lasted over three years. He had to go so I could survive.

As she worsened, I rose and did more for her. I'm no heroine and it was hard, but I would do it over again. I stood her up, often holding her for 45 minutes at a time. It wasn't easy. I found ways to help her walk. Moving my chair backwards, she leaned against it with her legs one-at-a-time forward. This kept her circulation going and muscles strong. These acts of love and closeness, I noticed such a beautiful, invisible, yet warm feeling of energy and goodness, like strands that connect an infant to their mother.

I asked the therapist what was wrong with me. Am I someone who can't cut the cords? She told me those are unique hormones that a mother gives to each child for trust and recognition prior to going through the birthing canal. I now discovered pure levels of Love existed. Love is stronger, conquers evil, and extends life. That's why love is such a powerful emotion and a level of consciousness. Per Amore = Quanto Amore. When you give out love, you get more back. I now understood what mom often tried to tell us. "If you can't do something with your heart, then don't do it at all."

It was a beautiful November day, unseasonably warm, sunny weather. The two of us went outside as usual, then Dysphasia showed me death at her door. I tried to hydrate her; the water caused her muscles to continue swallowing. It wouldn't stop. This time, alone in this tourist town, desolate, I picked her up without hesitation. Turned her sideways, swaying her in my arms as she did when I was little. It seemed to stop. At dinner time, while feeding her, the dysphagia resurfaced. We would be going back to the hospital.

I knew time was ticking but didn't know how long it would take. I looked up at the clear, warm, blue sky, pointed upward and said, "Today is a good day to die," in Bolognese. She communicated with me while passing. Within minutes, the doctor called while I was driving back to the hospital and said my mom passed. I fell to the ground and pounded my hand forcefully. Peace could not be present in Mom's final hours. Her last time with me. I went to the room to hug the bed, what was left of her energy and spirit. Startled, I screamed because under the sheets I felt her fragile, still body. I kissed her goodbye. I remember saying "I'm here mommy, I'm so sorry."

After my mother's death, memories. I realized I had lost my identity all these years. I was no longer a worker, a wife, a caregiver, a daughter. I couldn't bounce back and often had the idea of hanging myself over the balcony. I couldn't forgive myself, so I sought help from my therapist, who worked with caregivers. She said, "Why do you keep stabbing yourself? Can you caress your heart? What color is your pain?" I listened and replied when I could as she went on. "Can you bring it out? Can you let it go?"

My heart filled with so much shame, guilt, anger, apathy. I felt guilty for not being with her in her final moments. I have done almost everything I could until now.

My therapist said sometimes death is private, like going to the bathroom. People don't want you to remember them that way. Maybe they feel you won't let them go. She said you gave and saved her life so many times you wouldn't have let her go. Now, I began the healing process.

This gift of love was given to me, the caregiver. It brought a higher quality of life once I could recognize it. I evolved as a spiritual being through this higher frequency of love. Grieving shows us the depth of our love and can bring us a profound sense of peace and grace. Forgiveness is the greatest gift to me. Without this step, I would not have come to know who I am; I would have continued to live in the shadows of shame.

When we lean into love and connect with compassion, we transform and brighten one's life. Everyone experiences moments of magic. That is what my mom gave to me, Love.

"There were moments when it hurt so bad you couldn't breathe, yet somehow you survived the pain. There were days when you could barely put one foot in front of another, yet somehow you arrived at your destination. There were nights when you cried yourself to sleep, yet somehow you held on until the morning. Your life is nothing less than a miracle."

—ELEANOR BROWN

Margaret Whichard

Margaret is a Certified Substance Abuse Counselor, Mental Health Coach, Personal Life Coach and Chaplain. From an early age, she felt she didn't fit in and tried to fix herself. She realized other individuals had similar feelings. The need to help led to volunteer work with various churches and nonprofit organizations.

As a single mom, she strove hard to support her family. A late bloomer, she graduated college at 34 and was a mortgage banker for over 20 years. Volunteering was more fulfilling than mortgages. While most of her friends were retiring, she enrolled in college again to become a counselor.

As a counselor, her goal is to listen without judgement and accept clients as they are. She helps them explore their thoughts, feelings, and patterns; set goals; and develop healthy coping strategies.

Margaret discovered for her, the best way to heal was to help others heal. Margaret enjoys spending time with her children and grandchildren, reading, baking, and traveling.

MaggieMentalHealthCoach.com
margwhich@gmail.com (314) 956-2588

CHAPTER SEVEN

Hospital Frequent Flyer

MARGARET WHICHARD

"We're not sure we can save your leg or your life."

Alone, lying in this hospital bed, listening to the infectious disease doctor, I became overwhelmed with emotions. I caught my breath, my mind rambled and I could not believe what I was hearing. I was ready to meet God, but not today.

The thought of being an amputee was unbearable. I'm way too independent to hobble around or be bound to a wheelchair. This is not going to happen to me. Do I seriously have to learn to walk again at 65? A broken kneecap and multiple surgeries interrupted the path to my true calling. This was not my plan. Why is this happening to me? Determined to complete my requirements to be a Substance Abuse Counselor and I will walk again.

My right leg was in a full brace, my independence was gone, I never felt so helpless. In a dark moment, I asked, "Why do bad things happen to good people?" Infection ravaged my knee, and they were trying to keep it from spreading. If they didn't, it could be fatal. Oh dear! I imagined for a moment; I might die. Not this lady. Prayer chains began, and I put my faith in God.

The road to recovery would be a grueling one; 21 days at a rehab center. The first week, I didn't get out of bed. The staff handled most of my basic needs. It is quite difficult for an independent person like me. Every day, my heart stopped when the doctor came in to check my knee. My daughter took a picture. My knee looked like an overgrown rotten pumpkin spewing out its seeds.

It was December, and Christmas was approaching. I did my best to remain optimistic. Losing the ability to walk was an unbearable feeling. Like a child, I would need extra care.

I held my tears back in front of others. "Do I want to live if I can't hike or do Zumba and all the physical activities I enjoyed?" It's OK when your faith is weak, or if you question the things you do not understand, and even if you get angry. You might give up on yourself, but God never gives up on you.

When I returned to my home, I was anxious about how I would care for myself. It was very hard to ask for help. If only I could drive myself. Nine months later I had to learn new ways to do life. Most weeks, there were countless medical appointments. Since I couldn't drive, I relied on friends. I was always apologizing.

Peeking out the window, I could see the park where the seasons would change, and the leaves would fall to the ground. The midnight sky, crescent moon and stars rolled into the sunrise and still I sat and waited to heal. I was alone with no partner and life would never be the same. Out front was the car I couldn't drive. All I wanted was to go to Winnie's Tavern for a cheeseburger.

Just when I had some hope and life was looking better, it would fall apart once again. That stubborn infection, like an unwanted houseguest, haunted me. Oh no, not another surgery. The fifth surgery was the hardest, my longest hospitalization and the sickest

I had been. There were blood transfusions and massive amounts of antibiotics. Clinging to my faith, I wondered if this would be the time that I'd leave in a body bag. I dreaded each day, watching people come and go in the hospital and not everyone leaving alive. How much more time did I have on this earth?

Yet again, God helped me get through another dreadful episode and thankfully, the doctors said I could go home. They released me and cleared me to do "normal" activities. Normal? As the Black Sheep of the family, I had never felt normal.

Excited but scared, I immersed myself in work. I began my job as a Substance Abuse Counselor with a non-profit ministry. Unsteady on my feet I was grateful I could walk with the cane and always cautious because I did not want to fall again.

Work replaced the fun things I missed. My position was to provide counseling and support to homeless individuals displaced by Hurricane Florence. The goal was to provide housing first, then help them become responsible law-abiding tenants. They had multiple addictions, mental health issues, criminal records, health problems, little or no family support, few resources, and very little hope. They lost all their possessions in the storm. I don't know where I got the strength to do my tasks, but the energy carried me through. One day, I walked into a storm shelter to assess their needs, and compassion overwhelmed me. This was not what I envisioned my job to be.

The lack of housing compounded the distressing situation. I gasped for breath thinking how people must live in these horrible conditions. Some landlords agreed to rent the bedroom. As a counselor, I decided which individuals to place together. What a nightmare. Individuals with multiple problems, often strangers, current drug and alcohol users, others in various stages of recovery. There were some on probation, a few sex offenders, many with violent tendencies, and everyone traumatized by the storm needed housing. How was I going to safely place people and maneuver everything? I was not fully recovered when quickly, my work week grew to 60 plus hours. I pushed myself up the stairs even though it was a challenge. My problems seemed small compared to the lives I had to help. Maybe it gave me strength to carry on and motivation to heal?

Every workday was different. I had given up the comforts of corporate life, a regulated and predictable environment, to work with individuals considered unfit and unworthy. One day I entered a home through the kitchen and immediately smelled something different, an offensive smell. Glancing at the counter, I saw multiple empty boxes of cough medicine and dingy coffee filters. Something was cooking. Panic surged through me. "We'll reschedule later," I said while backing out the door. Normally a calm person, I fell apart before getting into my car. What had I gotten myself into when overwhelming tears took over and my stress released through every tear drop.

One day, a tenant called from a large house divided into three separate apartments. Living there were six residents with signed leases and an unspecified number of homeless individuals not on the lease. An intoxicated resident was upset with the woman living above him for stomping on the floor. He pushed her down the upstairs steps. When I arrived, a crowd had gathered on the front porch. "Oh, God," I prayed. As I approached, the upset tenant emerged with a pointed pistol. I had no idea what I was facing when I heard, "Miss Margaret, you've got to move someone else in upstairs so that I can get some sleep." Frozen with fear, attempting to be in control, I was relieved to see several cops hastily walking up behind me.

On the drive home, I asked myself again why I was having so many close death calls. Being honest, I admitted it was getting worse. I'd hit a stop sign, totaled my car, hit two mailboxes, had several falls, but what concerned me most was my cognitive decline. I could not continue living like this. The next accident might be my last. I was ready to seek help and look for a new job after spending Christmas with my kids.

Just outside the city limits, I checked on a client before leaving for the holidays. In the front yard, there was a large hog inside of a wire pen. "The latest addition to the family," she said. I kept a close eye on the hog as he pushed on the gate. Our time was up, and I headed to my car while the hog broke out. He was charging toward me, but I couldn't run because of my knee. You've got to be kidding. Last week it was drug dealers. Today it's a hog. God's Christmas gift to me was humor. On days when there was no reason to laugh, I thought of that hog and me desperately trying to get to my car. There was no doubt my occurrences were unbelievable, and I should write a book. I chuckled to myself.

My daughter was excited about showing me her new house. The family was training a new puppy and all the doors were closed. I opened the door to what I thought was the guest bedroom, but it was the basement. Taking a step forward, not even looking where I was going, I walked into thin air and flipped several times before landing at the bottom. My life flashed before me. "Jesus, I'm coming home." Immediately I went into shock. My lights were out when my daughter found me and called for help. The rescue squad transported me to the hospital where I'd been a patient many times in the past few years. The doctor joked, "You're a frequent flyer. Why are you having all these accidents?" CT scans revealed a collapsed lung, broken scapular, multiple rib, cervical and thoracic fractures. "Do you know how lucky you are? If you had hit your head instead of your shoulder, a little more this or that way, you could have been seriously incapacitated." Maybe God forgot to give me my wings or was training me to fly without them. It was all unreal.

A psychiatrist diagnosed me with mild cognitive impairment and PTSD. I had pushed myself almost to the point of no return. It was finally sinking in. Extensive lab work revealed leaky cells, brain inflammation, eight bacteria in my gut, and fungal overgrowth. The doctor recommended seven changes: quit my job, move closer to my children, reduce my stress, start exercising again, get more sleep, go to counseling, and work on my diet. I was staring death in the face, and I did not like what I saw.

As I thought about all my close calls to death, it was alarming how many there were in five years. Was I lucky, clumsy, blessed, or just stupid? Maybe I was crazy. Could I blame it on the jobs? My body was turning on me. It made little sense. I thought I was following my passion and doing God's work. Some friends said it was time that I stopped working, filed for disability, or claim my social security. I wasn't ready for that, but something had to change. I followed all the doctors' recommendations.

As a young adult, I felt God wanted me to do something for Him, but I ignored those feelings. I did not have enough faith in God or confidence in myself. My father was number 14 out of 14 children, with 35 ministers in that family. My sister and my son were also in the ministry. I did not want to join the family business.

Growing up in a strict fundamental home, I rebelled against all the rules I felt forced to follow. With every divorce, I felt unfit and ostracized from the church. Complicated would describe my relationship with God.

As a counselor, I could fulfill my desire to help others, give love, and comfortably share my faith when appropriate. But everything about this career transition was difficult. My health was at risk, and I continued to have potentially lethal accidents. There would always be more time, I thought, until one day I realized my time was almost up. God knocked me on my butt. What were the lessons that I needed to learn and what changes did I need to make? I constantly questioned myself.

For two years I have had no accidents, falls or near-death experiences. My health has dramatically improved. Finally, I learned to put my air mask on first. Being helpless forced me to accept help from others, something that is hard for independent women like me. Not working gave me the needed time to process many issues that had challenged me for years, leading to greater understanding and acceptance of myself. Often, I advise my clients to live in the moment while awkwardly trying to explain how to do this. Now I passionately share helpful hints sprinkled with examples from my life. I am a better counselor because of all that has happened to me. Not only is every day a gift, but so is every person. In my darkest moments, God was always with me. Infection wrecked my body. But God was holding my hand.

For a long time, I thought the life I was comfortable with was over. The old me had a lot of expectations about what I could, should, or would do. If you want God to laugh, tell him your plans. He has saved my life many times. Each miracle brought me more clarity. I needed to live to fulfill my purpose. If I survived the last five years, I could do anything! Never again will I risk my life by not taking care of myself first. Traveling is my favorite way to practice self-care. There are two states I have not been to. I plan to visit those and maybe a few foreign countries. Patiently, I'm waiting for God to replenish my bank account, and show me how my story will help others. God had given me wings to be myself. It's now time for me to fly.

"When life gives you lemons, make lemonade."

—Dale Carnegie

Irene Medina

Raised in Miami, FL. since the age of 3, Irene grew to love being around children and speaking about God. She spent much of her time in the church of Miami Bethany of Nazarene. Today she volunteers in the children's ministry at the church while working her full time job.

Growing up she loved to sing and write and would often find herself writing short poems or Haiku. In her spare time, she would bake mini treats with her family, and they would share with others the delicacies of low sugar treats.

Seeking to find her path and purpose, Irene had big dreams and wanted to finish medical school but changed her interest and decided to study social work. However, she noticed her emotions were a driving force for expressing her feelings and it became her passion for writing.

Irene has been drawn to learn more about writing and last year attended two writing retreats. This opportunity sparked her creativity. While working on a novel, she realized there was much to understand about the process of storytelling. When this opportunity presented itself, Irene wanted to share her story. It taught her greater insights for expressing herself authentically and inspiring others.

A new journey has emerged. Irene has her first published work now and plans on bringing more light to the world.

Irene.nalany2012@gmail.com
Facebook - @irene.medina.319

CHAPTER EIGHT

I'm Done

IRENE MEDINA

I had lived a lie!

My world was an illusion. Realizing years too late, I grasped on to a love with no sense of direction. The dreaded disappointments and heartbreak squandered precious moments. We never prepared plans or agreements to form a committed relationship. I struggled to know myself and never invested adequate thought into it. Everyday routines and obligations, and, like clockwork, I accomplished them. Always believing I'll never amount to my greatest potential in life, I lived in a fantasy.

A warm desire circulated within me and I delved into poems and read novels. I questioned myself, frequently wondering why I am saddened and shattered inside. Waves of emotions streamed through me like I had nothing else to live for; and all I had were obligations which didn't fulfill me.

We were teenagers, immature but yearning to be loved by someone. I dodged him most of the time. Since he usually preferred to skip school, I turned into his accountability partner. The good girl prompted me to drag him to class. Responsibility is invariably simple for me. I plunged right into the trap and never comprehended what would transpire.

During our moments together, we'd talk for hours; from family to ambitions, to places we wished to visit together. As time moved on, he assured me I would not have to worry about life or my future. A youthful woman, smitten and blind to what had actually taken place, I would lose myself to a lie.

Through time, I would create poems from my heart to support me through my process of pain.

"*Sent from Above*" –

"I thank God, he sent you to me, because you and I were meant to be. In you I found a love so true, it filled my heart with love for you. My love for you grows more with each passing day. Your gorgeous face takes my breath away. I dream of a day when we'll both say, "I do, for always and forever I will love you."

A wishful dream of a romantic teenager. I crumbled when he left me. Somewhere along the way, he moved to another state. I had lost my partner in crime. It appeared our dreams continued to die, though we chatted sporadically by phone or video, but it wasn't adequate. The confusion in my head had me powerless to concentrate on college, finding my way to 'fit in' and, ultimately, I had no direction in life. Life, an anxious ball of turmoil.

Growing up in a Christian church, I turned to prayer; I would constantly ask God to reveal the way and how I would serve others. A time came when the Pastor shared a sermon on how in the human world we don't hold as much value to our words. But in the spiritual world, it's like an unbreakable chain. Promises, which are simple words, are those chains? We crave to believe in promises but can be disillusioned when there no action behind them. At that moment, I remembered the promise we made to each other. Those words bound us together, like a pledge, but no action developed from them.

Years passed and other words and promises, but neither of us built this house on a stable foundation for a strong relationship; it dwindled down in the wet sand and slowly washed away with the waves of the ocean. I wonder how many young adults find themselves in the same situations. Could we avoid them if we had better self-esteem, healthier role models and clear communication with those nearest and dearest to us? Was it a part of growing up and why does it have to be so dreadful?

The prospect of being together sounded great, but I suspect now, we were confused, and this was not love. Perhaps our loneliness held us together. When I understood the words we spoke actually had no value, it intrigued me to understand this perplexing pursuit. I would soon be shown if the intent came from his heart and soul, a true love, or merely our own fear of loneliness.

Something changed when he received his diagnosis of a heart condition. That evening I wept for him, shedding tears from years of pent-up sentiments. He constantly tried to be a tough guy with others. Now he turned into a gentle person; showing how much he cared for me, wishing we would be together and tired of being alone.

When the phone rang, we chatted about the possibilities, and I asked a direct question: "Would you be willing to apologize and reconcile with my family before I make a commitment?" His remarks turned into anger. His stubbornness wouldn't allow him to apologize. My comments were unkind as well, because he deceived me and didn't respect the individuals I treasure most, my family.

Putting me in a position to choose him over family infuriated me, something I detest. There would be no further discussion.

Time passed by and the distance increased. Sporadically, he would reach out. This time I had a burning need to speak up and ask him, "Why did you stay in my life? Why not let me go?"

He simply replied, "You are untouchable, a challenge."

I practically dropped the phone from his reply. This was not the commitment response I desired. I had no voice for a minute. A chilling numbness engulfed me in the silence. My heart sank deep into a pit of depression, all a game, a hunt for him. The phone clicked.

That evening, I broke a chain. My prayer answered. We did not spiritually connect. While it terrified me to give up the only person who knew everything about me, I did not deserve the manner in which he treated me. He didn't judge me… or did he?

God sends different signs to us and when we listen, we learn, but I missed this one. The tears streamed continuously, my face in my pillow. I had no words for anyone. I needed to be left alone. "Why bother loving someone so intensely when you can't be together?" Love which hurts is not love. We didn't have the courage to declare, "We're done." So desperate and dysfunctional. Love doesn't hurt, we do, and unintentionally it hurts those closest to us.

This fantasy, like the princess stories we grew up with, never came true. The shoe didn't fit.

The day he died from a heart attack, everybody was in disbelief and shocked. I stood indifferent to those around me, laden with emptiness. I distanced myself. Church didn't interest me. I would pretend to have a smile, while slowly breaking inside. I wanted nothing and couldn't be with those around me and slipped away.

Now that he left, I was preoccupied with sadness, and I repeatedly asked, "Why didn't I let you go sooner?" My comfort and support was gone. He listened when I thought no one else did. I relied on him, but he couldn't give more than words of comfort. The warm embrace I required is no longer present. I still couldn't let go, though he left this world.

His heart failed and mine died along with it too. The pain he experienced in the end is not something I ever wished him to endure. I cried myself to sleep night after night. My room dismal and dark, as was I. Nothing made sense in this moment; emotionally, I was dying and couldn't escape the abyss I had collapsed into. Not knowing how to seek help, I didn't think I was worth lifting from the black hole I had created. I wandered in an endless cold labyrinth where I found my only solace.

Days after his death, the silence in my head became deafening. The tears had dried, but the numbness continued. I would constantly write poems, even if they were short phrases; like therapy, I turned to writing, and I discovered they were helpful.

I wrote this to him a few years ago; it remains true at this moment. "Tears are like rain. You cry when you're sad to release your emotions. It refreshes your body, mind, and soul. The rain does the same. It helps you feel happy, nostalgic, and free; it washes away the sorrow, sadness and the emptiness. You have one thing left: freedom.

We uncontrollably battered each other emotionally. My pain of losing you was destroying me, and I continued feeding those chains. They cut within like ragged edges of steel, sharp and left a scar. It caused me to feel worthless. For every other person who wanted to be in my world, I was not available.

Every day should be a fresh day, yet my heart still yearns for yesterday. I store my mind with reminders, knowing other ones will hurt to create.

Your voice is smooth, which many times whispered soft nothingness; your voice is now gone with the wind. The tender caress which once left goosebumps up and down my arm, your touch, is now a slow current, a subtle flutter in the wind. I heard your voice in the breeze today, as the beach waves soared high; its cool touch kissed my skin, never gone, never a goodbye. I listened to your cry, as I saw the storm come through. It blanketed me in its serene embrace, loving me in its warm hue."

I found healing in writing and music, my refuge. No one acknowledged the pain and the desolation within my eyes.

I needed to reach out for support and prayed every day for strength and comfort from my Heavenly Father. God had patience with me and dried my tears, the ones I didn't openly shed. He loves me when I turned my back on Him. Songs continued to pick me up during my storm. Words were more valuable and had newer meanings. I now understood.

The song "Praise You in This Storm" encouraged me to say, "I'm Done." Done with holding onto him; trying to satisfy everyone around me with smiles. I discovered myself through God; as the song played over on repeat, its messages were true. You, Lord, were constantly with me, awaiting me to turn towards You. You are the one who gives and takes away. It was his time, and he had to leave to put an end to suffering. I had to learn to surrender my pain and leave it in your hands.

"Tell Your Heart to Beat Again" by Danny Gokey, spoke to me. Did someone put these words before me for a reason? I didn't know how to piece them back together; yet, I had to understand to not live in the yesterday, not drown in the darkness that wanted me under. I had to look towards a new beginning. I had to let the Lord take the reins of my heart, let Him carry me, for He is with me.

Have you ever had a song knock the air right out of you? When I need healing most, God would always put the words for me to hear. Yes, words held more value each time. "You Say," by the artist Lauren Daigle, was another one of those moments when I couldn't hold back my emotions. When I was lost and couldn't find who I was, Lord, you showed me your love in different ways. I may sometimes feel like a failure, but my victories are in you. My self-worth and trust is in your hands, Lord.

We do not heal in one day, one month, or in one year. It takes one step at a time. The Lord gives and takes away. I will be alright; my wounds and scars may not be visible to others, but He sees them. Although this season of my life was emotionally draining, He uplifts me with love and patience and mercy every day. He is consistent, pursues me with fresh air in the morning; though I can't grasp why He loves me so much. It's amazing to find myself in His love; every day is a process.

I can now remember *him* and not feel my heart grow heavy with sorrow. I will never hear his voice again; but his suffering has stopped. I disappeared in his death, but by God's healing, I'm finding myself again. Drowning in the dark abyss, it suffocated me.

Blessings now overflowing, blessing other people, and showing them the true love of God in the middle of their darkness, of their storm.

I am done being my enemy; by putting myself down because I can't see my own value. I'm not a disappointment to God. Only He has the last say in my life. People can let me down, but He gives me life every day; in that life, He shows love towards me. God gave his life for me when I didn't deserve it. Yet He has His arms wide open every day, anxiously waiting for me.

I am done with everything, but I am not done with you, Father. Thank you for not being done with me.

"Whenever you feel unloved,
unimportant, or insecure,
remember to whom you belong."

—Ephesians 2:19-22

Linda Krider

Linda is a registered nurse by trade and an empath who lives in NC.

She is very active in church, and it was her faith in the creator that allowed her to rise above that experience. An inspirational speaker using her experiences to help others overcome negative thinking that often holds them back. It is her belief that each person has a purpose. When a person is called to a purpose, all they have to do is say yes. When one says yes to their divine purpose, they will find the creator aligning them with like-minded people who can help with achieving it.

Linda seeks to help people learn to overcome the fear that keeps them from saying yes to their divine purpose. In her spare time, she enjoys creating using resin, relaxing in the solitude of nature, and watching her grandchildren play sports.

lkrider.author@gmail.com
Facebook - Linda.Krider.Author
Linkedin - @linda-krider

CHAPTER NINE

When He Sees Me

LINDA KRIDER

This southern gal was tired of crying, being alone with very little sense of being worthy. Resting down in my bed night after night and praying. The blankets comforted me on the outside, but inside it was like being punished by a loving God. One palm ran into the other. The prayers began, me sniffling through every word. I did not understand why God created me this way, a damaged child? The thoughts should have dissipated by now, but it still haunts me as an adult. To top it all off, I now find myself in the midst of a divorce. "Please God. What did I do to deserve this kind of life? Explain to me what I did wrong?" Hoping each time for a response, never receiving one, I could not ease the sadness that poured through my words.

A mother births a child, pure of heart and soul. The child counting on the loving care to be cherished by her parents. They called me a bundle of joy. Cuddled after grueling hours of labor, she affectionately kissed me, lying on my mother's breast.

I constantly enjoyed when I heard the story from my mama. A child of God, a beautiful baby girl, began her journey on earth.

Little did this precious baby know the plans and challenges she would encounter.

My room was growing dim as the indigo night sky reflected through my window. Darkness resided inside my mind, emptiness and imperfection blocked the ability to shine my light. God doesn't create mistakes, I told myself. So why would he make me this way? Searching for many years, I needed an answer. I suppose we each have burdens to carry; I wanted to understand mine.

I recall it all, like yesterday. My first day of school in a little southern town. This little child, dressed by mama, delighted to make friends. There I paused, looking up at the huge wooden gates, seeming so tiny but proud inside to learn everything to be smart. What would I learn beyond those doors?

My eyes sparkled, my mouth grinned cheerfully, and if I could skip, I would gladly dance through those doors. Kindergarten is supposed to be fun. Kids get to play, learn, make crafts and play outside together.

This innocent child did not know what was facing her once her small hand pushed open the door to a different world. By the end of my first year, my way of life will change.

There were two teachers waiting to greet us. They seemed genuinely nice. The kids all running in, laughing and were ready to play. I was so happy as I hobbled over to a chair to sit down when she announced, "It's time for us to sit and introduce ourselves." I wanted to raise my hand first, but mama taught me to be polite and wait to be called upon.

We all looked around the room while I smiled at the new friends. The teachers were friendly and very thoughtful to me. Some kids looked sad. Maybe they missed their mom, I assumed. I was just happy to have someone to play with finally and learn lots of things.

My eyes wandered around the room while my teacher explained how our days would go. There was a place to hang our jackets, and each spot had our name above it. Along the top of the walls were pictures and letters. Like A for Apple. There was a beam of sunshine coming through the window and the dust particles floated through, virtually like they were dancing. I giggled to myself.

I saw one kid point at me and chuckle with another, but I paid him no mind. My parents used to tell me "Pay them no mind" when they noticed people looking at me. Not questioning it, I came to accept it as a way of life. Little did I know they were protecting me. Another little boy and I became friends and with played with one dolly.

When the day was over, mama had to slow me down from chatting too fast. Everything amazed me and I wanted her to know about all the fun things that I would get to experience. "Our teacher even read a book today, Mama," I excitedly blurted out. One day I imagined I might write something too.

Each night I would go to sleep merely to experience extreme pain. Putting my hand on my hip instinctively, I prayed it would go away. The suffering escalated over time and the shrieks penetrated the hallways of our little home. Why would God hurt me? I am not a bad girl. My heart shattering, breaking inside, puzzled why people would peer at me strange when I limped. I did not realize any of this made me different.

My family had to travel a great distance to bring me to the physician. On the way, I tuned into the fear my parents were going through, which made me frightened too. There were so many unknowns.

When I went in the examining area, a grouchy, silvery haired, wrinkled doctor with a gut decided my fate. He declared I needed to remain in the hospital for an extensive duration. I didn't want to be removed from my family. "Please don't leave me behind!" I screamed inside, terrified the doctors might keep me, and I would be alone. Moving away from him, I clutched my father's hand, looking up at him with apprehension and holding back tears. He knew I couldn't remain here, and he stood steadfast in finding another approach. Dad seemed like a strong man, firm and compassionate.

Tired of going to specialists prodding at me, following their eyes roll, their cheeks lifting while placing their hands on their chin, contemplating what to conclude. If they are so brilliant, why can't they not help me? I observed my parents' increasing concern and felt their love for me. Running or jumping with the other children was not possible! For a 6-year-old, this was devastating, but despite that, I still seemed normal. Indeed, my parents did not know what was happening to me.

It was tough for me to compete with the other kids in the playground. I showed my best. However, my limitations made it hard. We all stood on the grassy field. Kids were choosing teams to win while I remained there watching, hoping this time I would not be the last one chosen. My body hunched over, my head down, anxious they would not accept me again.

"You can have her." Those condescending remarks pierced through me every occasion I heard them. It crushed me to my core, never understanding why everyone else was excited and having fun while they mistreated me. It was painful to pretend I did not hear the hurtful actions people said. I suppressed my tears, determined to never let them notice me crying. I didn't want to be the victim falling apart inside. Maybe being tough and standing proud would stop them from upsetting me. Each incident it became harder to pretend.

I recall going to another clinic. I stepped in nervously because I knew today was the day. I would walk out with a brace. It was like the one Forrest Gump wore on his legs. Unlike his, mine did not bend at the knee because it had a part which stuck out past my foot. I had to swing my leg out to the side to walk. I was not looking forward to returning to school with this cumbersome thing strapped to my leg. If they were mean before, what would they do now that I looked different, too?

You can imagine I have heard nicknames. I would frequently get called things like "peg leg," "crip" or "hop along." It was truly heartbreaking. How come they were so cruel? I continued to hide my tears until I returned home. I can remember crying while telling my mom about it. She comforted by saying, "Well, it's not their fault. They have not been taught any better. It's how people are sometimes." Mama often spoke with incorrect grammar and a soft southern drawl. It was the way down here. Both my parents came from poor families and with little education. Mama was only eighteen when she had me.

It was not until third grade when I eventually got to ride a bicycle the correct way. Prior to then, I had learned to lay my brace between the handlebars and coast downhill and balance.

After many doctors' visits with multiple x-rays, I was told the disorder had been corrected, and the brace was no longer needed. One of the best days of my life was that one. I wanted to whoop with joy. I walked out of the doctor's office, smiling from ear to ear. I now looked like all the other children instead of a broken one.

My dad, stoic but always concerned, took me to another doctor. Afterwards, he was going to stop by the house before bringing me to school. While he was busy, I rode my bicycle. Finally, I had a sense of normalcy. Up and down the road I zoomed so fast, only stopping at the neighbor's house to show them I could ride. Later, I fell asleep, tired but happy. Dad saw me having such a good time, he did not have the heart to take me to school that day. I will always love my daddy for giving me that gift.

When I returned to school, I was nervous but excited. Would they finally see me and not my disability? I may not have had the physical restrictions with the brace off, but I learned that through the eyes of the other children, I was still the same broken person. I buried myself in books because it allowed me to go to another world and escape from the cruelty of life.

After graduating high school, I went to college and met a man I would marry. The warning signs were there, even then, but overlooked. He bought me flowers and other gifts and made me feel special. Three beautiful children, two sons and a daughter came from that union. I am grateful to them. After twelve years of an unhealthy relationship with limitations, I decided it was time for a change. I wanted us to have a safe and comfortable environment to grow up in.

Growing up Baptist with a father who was a deacon in the society and being taught the doctrines made it complicated to understand the things I was going through. When I found myself in the middle of a divorce, thinking I was guilty of something shameful and, like a failure, it made me feel like a disgrace to the church and God. I did not understand why God would want someone in an abusive relationship. I came to know that marriage may not always be forever.

I questioned my choices while I was learning how to be a better woman. Surely God would never use me if I did not have a purpose. Were my children my only reason to be alive? I made the choice to move to another church and not tell anyone my history for fear of what they would think. I would go to church and sit on the back pew and be one of the first ones out the door. Keeping to myself, I did not talk to people, avoiding eye contact.

I contemplated and wondered if I had a purpose. I slipped into depression and stayed in bed most days. I would lie awake hearing the voice that told me I was a failure. Repeated false accusations by others made me fear losing custody of the children. I still had them, and they were my purpose.

I heard a preacher say God could redeem us. Is it possible he would redeem me, too? Now at that moment, lying in bed with all the pent-up tears flowing down my face, and hoping he would answer my plea, "Please God. What did I do to deserve this kind of life? Tell me what I did wrong?" I heard him whisper, "What did my Son ever do to get what He got?" WOW! Did the creator of the universe just tell me that bad things sometimes happen to good people? I felt such forgiveness and love as he lovingly wrapped his arms around me and held me, just as any loving father would do.

He does not see me as the wretched, worthless person I believed. Nor does he see me as a broken child. God sees me as his beautiful, valuable creation.

The creator of the universe who hung the stars and the moon in the sky saw me as worthy of his love. When he created all the things in the galaxies and universe, he needed one of me. If God thought it important to create me, he must have thought of me as valuable. After all, he does not create anyone without a purpose. In the grand scheme of things, I may just be a speck, but God sees me. He sees me as worthy of his time and loves me unconditionally.

I would come to learn my purpose. To love people, uplift and encourage them. People who know me now may find it hard to believe I was ever quiet. I am the person standing up in front of crowds saying God loves us no matter our circumstances.

Just like the little teacup that must be molded, painted, and placed in the furnace before it can become a beautiful little vessel to be used; these things make us the beautiful masterpiece we are. That is how I imagine God sees me now as his beautiful creation.

"*No one can make you feel inferior without your consent. Never give it.*"

—Eleanor Roosevelt

Nicole Walker

Nicole Walker's professional trajectory includes twenty years as a subject matter expert in the global fragrance industry, predated by a decade of mentoring developmentally disabled adults. She a Certified Health Coach from the Institute of Integrative Nutrition, an honors graduate in Health Supportive Nutrition from the Institute of Culinary Education (NYC), a licensed Drugless Practitioner, and a graduate of the American Musical and Dramatic Academy.

Throughout her life, she has traveled extensively and has sought to explore the world as fully as possible; exploration which has fueled a burning sense of wonder and awe at the vast opportunities held within in every moment, situation, and relationship. She happily shares a 26-year marriage and a 20-year old son with her husband and describes their shared home as a "life lab".

Her personal mission statement is "to love fiercely, live kindly, and aspire to be an agent of positive change'.

Nicole Walker was previously published in PPP-Publishing's "*Awakening the Consciousness of Humanity*", edited, and with introduction, by Gloria Coppola.

This is Nicole Walker's second published piece.

To connect with Nicole, you are welcomed to mail her at
NicoleWalkerWellness@gmail.com or follow her
on Instagram at encouraging Nicole.

CHAPTER TEN

Facets of My Soul

NICOLE WALKER

I realize we've never met, and excuse me for sounding so bold, but... YOU ARE BEAUTIFUL!

A gem! With thousands of finely cut facets fashioned by God to accent your brilliance, I know this for a fact. How? Because God let me learn, I am HIS gem.

There are a thousand different ways we can learn, and God seems to recognize which approach is the most impactful. What I've grown to understand is, periodically, God sets up lessons in our lives about value and our perspective of it.

NO EVENT CAN UN-MAKE US

We were burglarized. Among the items stolen was my jewelry. Shimmering rings, dangle bracelets, pendants, earrings, all provided me with a sense of significance I did not notice it within myself.

Pieces that had taken their own generations-long journeys, woven with struggles, strengths and joys that came to serve as my family's heritage. Items acquired from the labor and experiences of my ancestors, who are coal miners, doctors, nurses, ship builders, soldiers, and holy men. Some pieces shrouded in mystery, with vague and distant stories of my Great Grandfather, a rabbi, fleeing the increasing persecution of his European home. These items, memorializing marriages, births, hardships, triumphs, and deaths. Gone. All gone.

Standing in our driveway, answering questions thrown at me by officers and detectives, I felt foolish, unnerved... violated. Stuttering through words while still struggling to process my emotions, neighbors gradually made their way to scope out the commotion. It embarrassed me. I wanted them gone. This was very personal and private.

My husband had not received the news yet. He didn't pick up his cell phone. I hope he won't ask me the same questions as the police. Did I lock the doors that day? Did I leave a window accessible by accident? We live in a modest home in a small town, with the windows at street level. Yes, I locked the doors and yes, all the windows were securely bolted shut.

A humiliating sense passed through even though I had done nothing wrong. Whoever this individual or people were, they broke in through our garage and, hidden from sight, applied a tire iron to pry open the steel fire door from garage to kitchen. The fire door we consistently keep bolted. So yes, I did everything right. I always did.

It was a beautiful spring morning when we left for school and work. We had recently replaced the front door lock over the weekend. The original one would stick, taking 10 minutes of persuasion and exasperation to turn. It was very aggravating, especially with an 8-year-old in tow.

Our newly sprouted lawn, a little overgrown, and our front walkway bushes neglected. Embarrassing, but only when I waved good morning to neighbors. I never found it simple to keep up with a white picket fence community, particularly since our fence is brown. Mentally overwhelmed, I am still figuring out how to manage a balance of work, family, appearances, and self-worth. I yearned internally to be carefree, like the white blossoms in my unkempt bushes.

At lunchtime, my wedding ring finger started to tingle. My hand had suddenly seemed naked; I hadn't worn my wedding rings that day. I don't have a clue why. But something appeared off. My pulse quickly raced through every vein; my gut unsettled. I swore I would slip on the rings tomorrow.

Arriving home, placing my hand on the front doorknob, that tingle zapped again. This time, my awareness bristled. That unsettled sense returned, but I didn't need my apprehension to squelch my son's playful smile as he observed. So, with the lead of his comfort, and a turn of the knob, we were safely home. A gentle sigh revived me. Everything looked the same. Hamster in its cage on the floor, the usual disarray of the living room… our haven.

We were barely home a minute when, "What the!!??" I froze at the door of the master bedroom… we would never leave stuff like this all over the floor. Dirty clothes and dust balls–yes-but not hair ties and spewed jewelry boxes. 'It's like something exploded in here'. My eyes became fixed on the crooked closet door that swung wide open. My heart raced further, gingerly treading closer, not knowing what I'd encounter. That tingling… it was legit.

"OH MY GOD, oh my God! Son, get out of the house. We've been robbed!" My voice shrieking in sheer hysteria. "Get Out!"

Scuffling my son out of his room, through the short hallway, unlocking the front door with ease and nudging us out onto the porch. "Shit. I didn't bring a phone," glancing up at the house from the walkway. "Mom, don't! They may still be inside." Now, my blood was flaring with a distinct sensation compared to the one from lunchtime. I went back in, hoping I would find someone, so I could… well… you know… hurt them. They weren't. Thank God.

'This was surreal,' snatching my cell and running back out again. A creeping awareness of vulnerability was slowly permeating my heart. Unfortunately, the feeling lingered relentlessly.

They took my wedding rings and all the rest of my jewelry, plus my son's laptop. Gratefully, they hadn't ransacked his room. That would have driven me lower. There was no need for it to be forever imbedded in the narrative of our lives. My thoughts dashed into the buildup of curious sensationalism I would face from acquaintances and co-workers who heard 'the news.'

You know, I've done this myself, asking insensitive questions under the guise of concern instead of extending consolation. Just like the neighbor who wandered up the driveway, with a demanding tone of "OK, what happened?" as if he were in charge. I turned my back. I didn't wish to see or hear him, because this time there wasn't the possibility of anything happening. It was real. I later understood he was scared, too. I don't blame him. I didn't have it in me to be bitter anymore that day. Now my energy was gone.

Why, God? Why did this happen? Why were we targeted? Who had the right to rummage through our home like a garage sale? They had more of a right to our belongings than we did? Did they work endless hours, putting away meager savings for something special? And after all they took, they likewise had the audacity to ransack 'our' master bedroom! They grabbed 'our' pillowcases to carry out our belongings. Pillowcases from the bed where we make love. Pillowcases from the place of midnight conversation whispered so as not to wake our son. This feeling of vulnerability is fierce.

On a material level, I knew they were merely objects. They were only items taken; we weren't physically harmed. I still have my family. Truth be told, I would have given 'this stuff' away if God had told me it would contribute to world peace. Except it wasn't given freely, it was taken, not by God, but by a nameless, faceless thief. And certainly, no peace in it.

It's all a blur, the aftermath. I was numb. Words, emotions, any conscious feelings were gone. I didn't want to live in my house, didn't need to talk to anyone, didn't choose to feel. I was apathetic.

This burglary had happened to my family, and I was becoming as much of a thief by robbing myself of myself. A double crime. Several days later, I looked in the mirror, not liking what was happening to me, who I was becoming. I realized at this moment I needed to heal. I called a priest to come bless our house. I desire the fear and anger gone.

Is anything more powerful than the violation of one's security? My answer: Yes, the Human Spirit. The human spirit can grow fiercer than a steel door or a gem. But this fierceness of spirit does not come overnight. It requires effort to show up.

USING EVENTS TO RE-MAKE OURSELVES

It was in the solemn part of my healing I imagined God, a skilled jeweler, holding me as a rare gem. A magnifying loop latched to His head, creating intricate facets; facets that only He and THIS gem would know. I had a choice; either be bitter and tarnish or find a way to renew my luster. No event can un-make us. I believe we can use events to re-make ourselves.

But how do you evolve from such guttural reactions of vulnerability and violation? I couldn't change what happened. It was done. What I had was choice and the power to transform my personal narrative. I didn't choose to witness myself as a victim because, intrinsically, we are more than that. That's how God created us. Nor did I wish my son's perception to be that someone else's actions could permanently define us.

Had I allowed myself to be violated throughout my life? Rarely listening to my gut inclinations. Remaining in harmful situations, fawning with fright. Like, the moment my former boyfriend called me a whore and backhanded me across the face because I didn't listen to him. Extremely frightened to defend myself. Instead, letting shame settle in and apologizing to him afterward. Never listening to my inner voice back then, yelling 'Get up, leave, be gone and never look back.'

I was training myself then; to be fearful, devaluing myself of credit, neglecting the discovery of my self-importance. I was going to learn a lot about what was valuable from this situation. I'm not certain there was a better way.

I thought about my Great Grandfather, the rabbi, the stories told of his beliefs and his love of the soul. His willingness to leave behind his home, a village of security, bringing along his wife, his children, his congregation. All to avoid persecution, with absolute bravery and faith in God and Man.

I am in NO way comparing my story to his. The point is this. This was my lineage, faith. So all those pieces of jewelry were souvenirs (souvenirs as used in the French way: memoirs). Yes, they had monetary value, but the real value was in bravery. The strength, will and love it represents can never be stolen unless we allow it to be. The real value was that I had all of this inside me. Already. My Great Grandfather understood. Just as God had faceted in me.

A jeweler never cuts a gem to decrease its value. A jeweler cuts a gem to increase its value. Every new facet makes it shine more, sparkle more, radiate more. Every new facet makes it more beautiful. Perhaps that's why we experience moments of vulnerability; to witness the beauty within our own souls and discover new strength and resilience.

Each of us, you and I, are vulnerable. And within these vulnerabilities are opportunities to discover new facets of ourselves. New strengths, new resilience, new beauty.

I'm still revealing new facets within my being. And in doing so, I discover more facets within others. Yes, I placed my trust in God, letting Him continue to polish me, but I also placed trust in myself. Entrusting in wisdom, God continues to teach me, appreciating that I am His jewel, the rarest of all kinds. I am beautiful; I am strong; I am resilient. I am fierce. And so are you. You are beautiful. I see you.

"And perhaps what made her beautiful was not her appearance or what she achieved, but in her love and in her courage, and her audacity to believe:

No matter the shadows around her, light ran wild within her, and that was the way she came alive, and it showed up in everything."

—Morgan Harper Nicols

Ann Marie Packard

Ann Marie Packard was born in San Francisco California. She's an Italophile, Italian food and wine retreat specialist, and postpartum doula.

When her father passed away at an early age, she traveled to Italy to heal her heart. During this trip, a dream formed, and Dolce Vita Retreats was born.

When she isn't wandering around Italy living la dolce vita (the sweet life), you can find her cuddling newborn babies or enjoying time with friends and family.

Are you dreaming of sipping your way through the Tuscan countryside?

Sign up for your own dolce vita adventure
with Ann Marie at DolceVitaRetreats.com
info@dolcevitaretreats.com

CHAPTER ELEVEN

The End of Innocence

ANN MARIE PACKARD

In the summer of 1983, I was an independent, naïve 13-year-old facing a decision many teens confront when there is conflict at home: accept the punishment, run away or worse.

After a fight with my mother, I packed a suitcase, wrote a heartfelt goodbye letter to my father, placed it on my pillow, and crept out the door after my parents fell asleep. What I wanted more than anything was for my mother to try to understand me, to talk with me and not be so rigid. I wanted to be heard and feel that she cared for me.

Some may consider my mother neglectful. I was called a latchkey kid, taking care of myself from age five. The authorities had removed my older sister from our home before I was born, because of evidence of abuse. Though I now realize my mother was suffering from her own demons, as a little girl I knew only that she was cold toward me and acted like she didn't want me or my sister.

My dad was my confidante. He was traumatized from losing one daughter and so kept a watchful eye over me. But he didn't have the strength to govern the family or make a home that was safe.

The sky was a deep indigo when I arrived at a friend's house around midnight. I attempted not to panic when she didn't answer the door. Glancing around the neighborhood, I walked to a pay-phone and decided to call my boyfriend's uncle. He had offered shelter when I ran away once before.

My parents allowed me to go on dates at a young age under the condition my boyfriend's uncle chaperone us. I doubt they realized he was only 21-years old. He didn't look it with his height and weight and facial hair. What they also didn't know was he was dealing drugs. He gave us tiny envelopes of cocaine to give out to our friends.

When he answered the phone, he was happy to hear from me. I asked for help. He obliged and told me he would come soon. Within thirty minutes, he picked me up.

He owned a business with an apartment at the back. He told me I could stay as long as I needed. A sense of safety made my pulsing heart calm down. It wasn't the best living arrangement, but I wouldn't be out in the cold and alone.

Life was fun for the first couple of weeks. But then my boyfriend, who was away all summer, broke up with me. I learned years later that his uncle threatened to break his arm if he didn't break up with me.

In the meantime, I was quickly becoming popular as I continued giving out the tiny white envelopes. Luckily, drugs were never an issue for me.

Before I ran away, my father had given me the *Drug Talk* during one of our usual evening chats while my mom watched TV downstairs. He warned me that I was getting to an age when people might start offering me drugs. He said he knew I might be curious and that I may even try some.

"If you really want to try something, go ahead, BUT if you don't like it, never do it again. If anyone teases you, look them right in the eye and say, 'I tried it and I don't like it.' Don't be afraid to stand up for yourself. Remember, anyone who tries to force you to do something you don't want to do is not your friend."

This was an important lesson, but one I didn't yet know how to apply to other situations. During our talk, I saw the pain in my father's eyes as he shared a story of his cousin that committed suicide during a bad drug trip. I loved and trusted my dad. He was a gentle and compassionate person. Never a doubt he didn't love me. I would take his wisdom with me.

I tried marijuana, hash, and cocaine. I thought snorting cocaine up my nose was gross. Pot just made me hungry and sleepy. There was no allure for me in any of it. I heard my father's words in my head, remembered him telling me about his cousin's suicide. When a friend did tease me about not getting high, I stood up for myself. It felt empowering.

In September, I planned to show up on what would've been my first day of eighth grade, determined to make the honor roll. Attending college on a scholarship was my goal. My first dose of reality hit hard when I found the police were looking for me. School was no longer an option. My dreams were shattered.

I was raised a "good Catholic girl." I wanted to save myself for marriage, or at least someone I loved.

The "uncle" took care of me. He bought me clothes and gifts, took me out to fancy dinners. Looking back, I realize he was grooming me. It was all a manipulation. He had an ulterior motive.

One evening, he took me into his office and asked me to sit on his lap. My stomach felt uneasy, and a lump of fear in my chest made it hard for me to breathe. But I did as he said. What happened next was not what I would have ever imagined. It would become the memory of *My First Time*. He would rob me of my innocence.

Noting my nervousness, he teased me, pulling me close as he flirtatiously asked me to have sex with him. My eyes widened, as my breath stopped. I was afraid to move. "But you're like an uncle to me," I managed to utter. I was trying to be nice, something my mother had taught me. "Be nice!" she used to say, instructing me to hug whatever "uncle" was around, creepy or otherwise. "Don't be rude."

"You have to pay me back for the drugs, clothes, food and shelter I provided you all this time. I've done a lot for you."

I was stunned. "But… I don't have any money, or any way to work," I explained. I was apologizing now, feeling responsible for *owing him.*

His next words would live within my cells forever: "Don't worry about money. There are other ways you can pay me."

It was obvious what he was insinuating. Tears rolled down my face while he touched me, but I remained silent. I felt sick about it. But I thought I was obligated.

I closed my eyes, praying it would be over soon and I wouldn't have to do it again. Afterwards, I was shaking. Blood stained the sheets. It hurt. I felt sickened and overcome with guilt and shame. I wanted to run away but had nowhere to go. I kept my secret.

When the first opportunity came to leave for a safe place, I went to a girlfriend's house. He called relentlessly. I didn't want to talk to him, but he yelled and insisted. He was irrational, accusing me of cheating on him and threatening me. My heart was pounding, my mind racing. My friend and I were terrified. But I didn't call the police because I was also fearful to go home. In my 13-year-old mind, I believed anywhere was better than home facing the anger of my mother.

Moments later, I was in his truck cowering against the passenger door as he screamed and shook his fist above me, his eyes wild with rage.

"I'm sorry," I kept repeating, holding my arms up to protect myself and moving my face away from him. He drove straight to a motel, slamming the door behind us. He acted insane.

I was frozen, watching him alternate from punching himself in the head, to slamming the bathroom door against it. He proceeded to lay on the ground exhaustedly knocking his head against the floor, all the while yelling, throwing things, accusing me of trying to leave him, and crying. Utterly bewildered and believing that *I had hurt him*, I promised not to leave again, repeating "I'm sorry, please stop hurting yourself."

Around 3 o'clock in the morning he insisted, "Come with me to Connecticut!" I agreed so he would stop hurting himself. He quickly packed, and we left. I had no idea what else I could do, it seemed like my only option.

Halfway across the Golden Gate Bridge, I summoned the courage to say, "I don't want to go, I don't want to leave San Francisco."

His wicked response evoked a deep fear within me. "Where are you going to go? Home to your mother?" He pressed hard on the gas pedal. We were already going over the speed limit. "Go ahead, jump," he dared me. I had no choice, no hope. I clung to the door, hot tears flowed soaking my neck. I didn't say another word.

My period never came and by my 14th birthday, I knew I was pregnant and could never go home again. I acclimated to my new life, believing I had no way out. He opened a lock shop in town where I learned the valuable skills of running a business, scheduling, and bookkeeping. This would one day provide me with a business foundation for my future.

By the age of 16, I had two children. A friend detected something wrong and helped me seek the advice of a lawyer. But the legal system failed me, resulting in losing contact with my daughters for fourteen years.

The emotional abuse and humiliation I endured for three and a half years before I escaped and made it home to California, was traumatizing. Separated from my children whom I loved and missed, I cried every day. I was young and easily manipulated. But I don't consider myself a victim. I made mistakes. But overcoming and learning from them is how I learned resilience. I wanted to be there for my children. But first I had to adjust and get help.

I began to put my life back together. I took classes at a community college, read self-help books, learned to make self-care a priority, sought therapy, got certified in a positive psychology coaching course at a local university, and dove into spiritual healing.

I learned that we attract people who present issues we need to face, people who ultimately help us work through our issues. Those difficult relationships were a necessary step in my growth process. I married and had three children. I was still healing, though, and those years were not easy for my children to navigate alongside me. It created chaos and a loss of trust and respect.

But now, my children are adults. I see how all of us suffered, how all of us need compassion and healing. I had always wanted my own mother to communicate with me and provide a sense of safety. It is hard to imagine what my children went through. But I continue to work on mending our relationships and showing up for them today.

There are still triggers, but I can navigate them more easily. I've dealt with depression and feelings of hopelessness. But I continued to push through each lesson, learning to forgive as I moved through the trauma to create my best life.

The day I made the Dean's List at City College of San Francisco was one of my most empowering moments. I know that I cannot change what happened to me and what I did in the past, but I can work to create a life I could only once have dreamt of. I learned you can overcome trauma and create the life you want, no matter what has happened to you.

Past struggles and traumas didn't define who I was. But overcoming them has helped me to find my voice, to say *"no"* to things that don't feel right. I have learned to trust myself and follow my intuition. In the past, I often did things to appease others. Now, I know that if I pause and pay attention, things can align. It takes diligence and commitment to learn new patterns.

The most powerful healing moment I have experienced was at a women's retreat I attended just after my 50th birthday. During a Reiki and EFT tapping session, the practitioner helped me go back to my earliest memories and apologize to that little girl for not protecting her. I made a new promise to do so from that day forward.

I almost blew off the session, but everything kept putting it in my path. The universe speaks to you if you listen. I'm so glad I did. I believe I am drawn to these ways of healing in order to look at the generational trauma that needs healing.

After my children were grown, I created a new dream for myself pursuing my passions. I founded a retreat business. Since I knew many of the basics of running a business thanks to everything I survived, I realized I was capable. I have done more than survive, I have thrived!

I began traveling to Italy every year which fed my soul. Later, I founded a food and wine retreat business, sharing my joy and knowledge with others. I also have become a certified postpartum doula. Caring for babies through the night fills my heart. I give the families of newborns that I work with the rest they need. It is my hope they will be able to build solid parent-child relationships, something I have always longed for. I have come full circle in this regard. It's interesting how we find our purpose. I created the best of two worlds -- the love of family and showing people my heart home, Italy.

When my mother died, I was by her side as she took her last breath. I anointed her chest with rose oil to ease her transition and forgave her as I grieved the mother-daughter relationship, not only ours, but the one she didn't have growing up, and the one missing with my own children.

I can now see the healing needed to end the cycle for my grandchildren.

Writing this story has been very cathartic. I uncovered new areas of forgiveness, not only for my mother, but also for the man who took away my innocence, and most importantly, for myself.

It is my hope that sharing this small glimpse into my story can help you find or amplify your voice and serve to help you mend your own parent-child relationships.

I had no idea how *Women Standing Strong Together* would provide me with the healing insights by sharing this story with you. We all need strong women in our life.

"Trauma freezes the memory narrative. It is the task of the survivors of early childhood trauma to thaw out and turn it into a story."

—Lyn Barrett

Chrisanthi Voukatidis

Chrisanthi is a woman born in Sao Paulo, Brazil, later moving to Michigan. She began her adult career immersed in a family business. With an apprenticeship in Beverly Hills, California, she developed her craft as a hairdresser.

Eventually, her love of the ocean and faraway places set her on a seven-year journey as a guest relations manager aboard cruise ships. This journey took her around the globe showing her the wonders of the world and the wonders of humanity.

Ultimately, she decided to plant roots on land, focusing on family and by learning the healing arts. She began to build a new career as a massage therapist, immersing herself in the healing arts. A ten-year journey that led her to continuously learn and develop her skills the ancient healing modalities of Hawaiian Lomilomi, as well as Thai massage. Her fascination with integrating healing of the mind, body, and spirit led her to study and work throughout the world. Until suddenly, life put her on a life-altering path presenting her with the ultimate challenge. Calling her to heal and transform herself.

"Healer, heal thyself."

cvlambo@gmail.com

CHAPTER TWELVE

Coming Home

CHRISANTHI VOUKATIDIS

"At last! Bone of my bone and flesh of my flesh."

Immediately he recognized her and called her Woman.

God's gift to man, exemplifying the extraordinary essence of love.

Naked and elegant, created to love and be cherished.

Craving union with him, the body from where she was formed.

Immersed in bliss as their two bodies merge back into one.

Glowing from their union, designed to nurture and bring forth life from her womb.

Overflowed with wonder and joy in God's glorious garden, a Paradise to expand and enjoy. Living eternally in God's frequency of love.

Disastrously, evil slithered in, telling her lies.

She listened and believed the lie.

Lies lead to catastrophic loss and agony.

The Pleasures in Paradise, perhaps a few. Splendid bodies would now disintegrate back into the earth.

As a young girl, I always knew I was loved, protected, and held with a strong sense of family support and encouraged to pursue my dreams. They prepared me to find an appropriate man and share life with him, but not to depend on him to survive or be happy.

There were never limitations imposed upon me or rigid indoctrinations. Some individuals grow up with that, forcing them to accept certain guidelines, like marrying young or creating a big family. Many women not encouraged to have a career, or pursue higher education and, thus, I gained more power. Strong in my mind, my body, and confident in my skin.

My parents lead by example. In my mother, I see the personification of the divine feminine woman. A physically and internally graceful lady, capable of loving and being secure. She showed her daughters, with Jehovah, all things are possible.

Staring up into her beautiful eyes, my heart would connect with hers and I recall being in admiration. I still am because she gave me the courage and confidence to follow my dreams and listen to the passion within myself. But like Adam and Eve, I am not proud of all decisions made in my life and have been drawn by false promises. Many I have traveled down were dangerous paths and lost sight of my true power. Paradise was lost.

From his rib, powerful enough to protect breath and love, God created her. From him and for him, she would be his helper, his companion, complimenting and completing him. Perfect bodies enjoying nature's full buffet. Simultaneously, they would be fruitful, and all living things would be born through her. Woman, God's gift to man.

Oh, how I revel in that part of the story. Perhaps, taken out of context on some occasions.

Unfortunately, their state of bliss would be short-lived and would quickly face the harsh realities waiting for them when the forbidden fruit led them astray from the Creator.

Naturally, we are designed to love and be loved. Just like in the bible, we have been tempted and led away by deception. Yearning for a deep unconditional union of two souls, a companion to experience the adventures of life and have a family. Like a fantasy movie, I would be swept away one day and drenched in blissful moments. But would it be the expression of God's love? Not quite I came to learn.

One day, I packed up and planted my feet, soon to marry the man of my dreams. We reinforced each other's ambitions and set up a new life. It was an amazing time in my life... until it wasn't. Instead of celebrating our accomplishments, we grew apart. What had we missed? The devil continued drawing closer, breathing down our backs and forcing us further apart. Distractions and solitude increased the distance. I was losing sight of my steps and seeking outward for love instead of towards God.

My foundation was uncertain and all I managed to do was put one foot in front of the other. Extra armor protected me as I walked on with my heart broken and spirit crushed.

I remain before you, God, in front of this splendid ocean you created, melting into the sand, and listening for you to guide me. Have you ever received a love so grand that rays of light comforted you, the wind hugging you and playing a charming melody to your ears? The salty air kissed my lips and there it was. Love. God's glorious love. A frequency I practically missed, so healing, it repairs my broken heart. A dimension of grace and beauty produced tears to my eyes filled with joy.

All I could do was Praise Jah. Minutes turned into hours, and my body became lighter and brighter. I was returning and re-remembering who I was. It seemed as if things were getting better and, in the blink of an eye, disaster struck.

Catapulted into a new reality. The things that had previously kept me crying and awake at night abruptly turned into something so small and irrelevant. A life-changing, fatal motorcycle accident flung me off an overpass and up into the air, sending me crashing 44 feet to the ground. As if the evil one himself flicked me off the overpass, to attack, test, and destroy. God sent his angels to soften the fall. Virtually all my bones are broken, vertebrates shattered, leaving my organs and spinal cord damaged. The earth was embedded deep within my broken bones, exposed because of the flesh that had burnt off. Laying at death's doorstep. My body was kept together by skin, ligaments, and tendons. The breath of God was sustaining me.

Not understanding what was transpiring or why, did I neglect to trust God? Feeling sorry for myself, empty and not in harmony with my brain or heart. The full union I long for created a void in my heart. But why today? He was with me at the ocean; I knew it.

Piercing sounds panicked and confused me, the raw shrieks of a wild animal struggling to survive and escape. Terror raced throughout my veins, losing it as I realized I was that wild animal. Everything was moving so rapidly, people rushing and shouting, informing me I was in the hospital. "NO! NO!" Agitated and delirious, I continued screaming at the top of my lungs. We hurried down corridors and into elevators, passed from arms to arms, seeking desperately to understand what was taking place and frantically wanting to escape. "Let me go, let me go! I'm strong!" I heard a voice say, "Let her try." I struggled to run away but was completely paralyzed. Recognizing I couldn't even move a finger, I didn't know where my finger was, or if I had one. "Oh, God!"

Days passed as I drifted in and out of consciousness. Until the screams began. My skeleton was held together by titanium. My frame was bound and attached to the bed. Tubes and bags hooked up to my organs and the excruciating agony had me counting the minutes until the elixir was injected deep into my veins, loosening the agony's grip, if only for a while. Each time I pleaded for more, but more would cause my heart to stop beating.

Death seemed merciful. Longing for that deep sleep, secure in knowing my King, Jesus Christ, had shed his blood to pay the price and conquered death. A life in agony, confined to a bed or chair, and needing to be cared for like an infant was terrifying to me. How easy it would be to close my eyes in a deep sleep, waiting for my Savior to resurrect me. Yet, I knew better, for God had kept me alive.

Crippled in pain, fear looming overhead, ready to swoop down and devour me like flocks of vultures. I cried out. In Jesus' name, please, Jehovah God, take me, your wounded child and embrace me in your arms! Please carry me. Surround me with your angels and fill me with your Holy Spirit. Give me strength beyond what is normal, peace beyond the pain. In Jesus' name, have mercy on me, Father.

God acknowledged my prayers. His voice echoed in my mind, telling me to surrender. His Holy Spirit flowed throughout my shattered body. A golden light enveloped me as I felt softer. My heart beat strong, sending vibrations and light pulsating, like an electrical current traveling throughout my bones and blood. My mind's eye gazes deep into the darkness until it breaks free into flickers of light, sending energy of love and healing to every cell. A symphony of sounds carried me into a frequency of love.

I trusted in Jehovah, knowing we would face whatever would be. Glancing outside the window, my mind traveled with the ever-changing clouds showing me how simple it is to flow and transform. I would close my eyes, pray. My mind's eye would detach my soul from the confines of my body and flow into a field of vibration and light.

"Yes. You who created me in my mother's womb. I will praise You, for I am fearfully and wonderfully made. Marvelous are your works. And this my soul knows very well." It overwhelmed me with gratitude for God's mercy and grace. Days passed into weeks, and weeks turned into months. One operation led to another, quickly leading up to ten, then twenty, leading to thirty. The reality of that physical experience of having my body reconstructed leaves me dumbfounded.

Years have passed since April 2018. I dedicated every day since then to reclaiming and empowering my new body. Almost as if experiencing death and rebirth. Recreating myself, and learning patience and love, for this new body that has experienced radical transformation. Mourning the loss of the strong and graceful body that it once was. This new body moves slowly, cautiously, calculating, and counting every step. Each day adding a new movement to the dance, exhilarating and painful, growing and slowly regaining strength.

Appearing to be fragile, many times requiring rest and recovery. Yet, fueled by God's gift of strength and resilience. My body moves by sheer will, determination, and the grace of God. The process of creation is slow and often agonizing. Pain is a nagging and many times a cruel companion. The only balm powerful enough to soothe and to ease the pain is the power of love. Just as a woman can birth a child and endure the pain eased by God's love, I have also experienced the ease of flowing, and feeling the vibration and light.

I am continuously lathered in the healing balm. Progress has been like the speed of molasses. Baby steps but steps none the less. I celebrate every small victory. Finally, having learned where and how to intimately merge with my Creator and dance in His symphony of love. My heart and soul settled into my new home. Surrounded with support and love. On the other side of the pain, I found peace, secure knowing I am loved. God's glorious love means something more profound to me now.

During my darkest days, I almost didn't want to open my eyes anymore, wondering how the sun would ever shine on me again. Today, I feel the sunshine on my skin. I am alive! Amazed and proud of myself for having never given up on limitations about my body.

When I was paralyzed, I felt the energy, light, and vibration traveling throughout my body. I trusted in God to give me the power necessary to endure whatever was necessary to get through the most difficult of times. "Praising Jah, for I am fearfully and wonderfully made." Love gave me the courage to push past my limits, to live a life that reflected the gratitude I felt for receiving the precious gifts of love, peace, and security. Thanking God for filling me with His Holy Spirit. Inspiring me to grow, create, love and be loved. It was then I understood the divine feminine and how creation was designed.

I am a woman, just like the strong and loving women that surround and inspire me. When faced with difficult circumstances, the women I know have risen above and overcame them, becoming better than they were before. I could do no less.

I am a woman creating a better world around me.

I am a woman who loves differently now and is deeply loved.

I am a woman who looks to my Creator, connected with my source of power. Neither man nor circumstance can take that from me.

Man formed from dust.

Woman made from the rib of man.

Indeed, a gift from God. The wisdom gifted to me.

Yes, I am Woman.

"*Love bears all things,
believes all things, hopes all things,
endures all things. Love never fails.*"

—1 CORINTHIANS 13:7

Judy Warner

Living in South Carolina, raised in the Midwest, third of five children. Three grown children and three grandchildren. I have a love of books and writing was encouraged and nurtured by my oldest brother, Jim. Library days at school I would be found in the corner reading Little House in the Big Woods and Caddy Woodlawn.

The words brought my imagination to paper where I would rewrite the endings of tv shows to favor the underdog.

I worked in manufacturing sales for twenty years, leaving after the job had devoured my soul, returning to school to be licensed massage therapist, where my intuitive abilities expanded through Reiki working with clients in chronic pain.

Always having a wanderlust, I love traveling across the US and overseas. Most of my time traveling between grandchildren, watching them grow and mature.

My bliss is hiking the mountains and laying on the beaches, enjoying earth and skies energies.

judy.warner01@gmail.com

CHAPTER THIRTEEN

Dancing Lights

JUDY WARNER

Dancing lights of gold and pink would wake me at night. Despite their whimsical nature, I was terrified when they would show up. First, I would feel a presence. Waves of energy like soft breezes would float around the bed. As I peeped from underneath the sheets, my eyes popping like a cartoon character, my heart pounding in my chest and unable to breathe. Further down into the blankets I would tremble, until I would race from my bed, stumbling over the covers on the path to the door.

Oh my God, I cannot stand it, help me God. What is happening to me? Please God, take this away from me!

As I nudged the door wide, it smashed against the wall behind it. My brothers had to be playing tricks on me. At least, I assumed.

"Dad! The boys are up here scaring me with their flashlights. Make them stop."

My dad snickered, "The boys are down here, completing homework. Go back to bed, quit banging the doors. You will wake the baby! There are no lights in your bedroom."

His remarks hurt me because he didn't believe me. Drawing the covers over my head, feeling my breath against my pillow, I held the tiny pink rosary. The pink beads rolled between my fingers, praying, "Dear Jesus, take this away from me." He did not.

Born a natural empath and psychic, I experienced many unexplained anomalies. When I was young to these events, I did not understand. One day I learned a responsibility to myself, regardless of what the spirit wishes.

Along with the ability to detect someone's anxiety, emotions, depression, I have a gift to pick up energy in spaces and buildings. When I enter a space or touch an individual, it's like a movie downloaded into my mind. Information plays out with precise detail. This intensifies my anxiety.

Praying incessantly, my continual mantra hoped to eliminate the visions. I struggled to block the energy by removing myself from it. With no understanding how to manage this ability, I became physically ill.

Sometimes the intensity would become too much for me to breathe. Imagine someone wrapping me in plastic with nowhere to escape. Hiding in the flowering bushes around our home comforted me. My anxiety, and the energies evaporated into the earth. Had I intuitively diffused the energy and ground myself?

The birds accompanied me in the flowers, their wings would sweep against my cheek. As we sat fascinated in an enchanted dance, the gold and pink lights would swirl between the white fragrant flowers, and the emerald green leaves providing me inner peace. Anxieties at bay here, my solace away from the dysfunctional family. The pure joy in that area was delightful and comforting.

When I mentioned to people I recalled being born into this life, they did not always receive it well. Imagine you have the capacity to see what is happening before you enter this world. I watched my mom before my delivery as she was being prepped for my birth. The stark white walls with ceiling to floor windows draped in faded curtains were a contrast to the dark framed bed occupied by mom. Next to me, a presence. It reminded me of a grandmothers' hug, unconditional love urging me telepathically to enter the room. I preferred to stay in the presence, as if I was pleading. As I approached the bed, in an instant, I was being propelled from my mother's vagina. Chilled from the warmth of her womb, they suddenly swaddled me in heated blankets and towels. Followed by a brisk disengagement from my mother and whisked off to a small transparent box which was extremely warm.

My next recollection was being held in my dad's arms at my baptism. The wool from his gray sports coat scratched my face as the priest walked to the baptismal fount. His enormous belly and the smell of a stogy tickled my throat, and I coughed. The priest glanced at me, "She looks blue." Concerned, these remarks pierced my dad's heart, thus being filled with panic. Passing me immediately to my mom, I sensed great sadness.

Everybody has the ability, and some go off in the directions, not the safest. Specifically, those who don't understand boundaries. One may not realize how to switch it off and can get depleted. You are a portal, understand? Open for anyone to enter if you are vulnerable.

I remember watching children who had crossed. They showed me where they were. I knew they called for help. When I spoke with the police, I was able to identify the name of the attacker. When they discovered the child on a riverbank, the way it appeared to me, I recognized I had to protect myself. Mediums are known to connect with souls who have passed. While it is an amazing gift, it wasn't something I was ready to accept.

The initial decision I carried out was to stop providing massage therapy. The connection is so intimate, I would receive information and later I couldn't sleep. It's too extreme for one to handle.

Soon, I would learn to listen and trust my instinct to protect myself. We have free will to determine what we want. Reading books and attending trainings helped me better understand and use tools to protect my energy.

Boundaries: Goal

Information overflowed through me rapidly, and it was never simple to stop it. Being a clear vessel requires discernment.

Surround myself in white light. One of the simplest means I would come to learn and master.

The true essence of God is in the moment of divine love. Nothing harmful will penetrate.

I would discover the power behind this gift one day.

One day I was going to work and had a lengthy ride. Abruptly, I realized I did not have my cell phone when I was urged to turn back home. Why did I insist on having my phone?

Before I left work in the evening, I went to use the ladies room. The lights hovered over my head. *They were back.* "It's about me." Those words lingered in my mind while I recalled my nephew's drowning the previous year. My heart raced, knowing he was trying to give me a message.

When I unlocked my car door and scooted into the driver's seat, I noticed a presence around me. My nephew who passed and a friend who died in a car accident were in the rear seat, sitting quietly.

"What are you doing here?"

"You will need us."

My pulse was swiftly escalating. OMG, what was happening?

The drive home caused tension. I kept my focus at a coffee shop by the corner. The light turned red when I slammed on my brakes at the intersection. The car behind me wasn't paying attention and struck so forcefully into my car, it propelled me out into the intersection. Everything was developing so rapidly. In the corner of my eyes, I noted a semi-truck approaching! With no time to do anything but express, "Your will be done, please. Please protect me."

Bam, my head struck the windshield as the semi-truck plunged into the car. Somehow, my body went to the back seat with my friends.

"It will be over soon."

My spirit was leaving my body when I became aware of absolute love. Even though I saw myself sitting in the driver's seat while staring down from above the crushed vehicle there was no fear.

All I thought of was my parents. My nephew passing 6 months prior, my parents would not handle this if I leave.

My uncle, who was close to me (on the spirit side), held my hand. "I'm so happy you are here. I'm always here."

I detected the pipe aroma, see his ruddy complexion and freckles. He wore plaid shirts, deep purple and gold. There he was outside the car door.

I slipped back into my body.

There was a loud sound, sirens. "Remember, I'm with you all the time." Peace was all I felt.

Fear and dying no longer existed. Immense love from all three of them surrounded me. The ambulance appeared promptly.

Now I realized why I went home to pick up my cell phone. My son needed to know about the accident and where it happened.

"OMG, are you ok?"

Barely a murmur came out, but sufficient to speak a few words to him. "My neck is restrained. I'm on a body board."

The emergency responders moved hurriedly, and I drifted into altered states of consciousness as they calmed me down.

There was no concern as they dashed through the main door, flew down the hallways, working as fast as they could to scan my brain and spine. I heard faint voices from the medical team in a distant consciousness, while I dropped in and out of pain and love.

A deep voice with concern said, "She will never walk again. The damage to her cervical and thoracic spine will be impossible to heal."

"You don't know me very well," I whispered. "I'm going to walk again."

One month later, I received intensive neurological care in the hospital, living in intense pain daily. It was then I recalled someone who didn't really like me at all. I had no boundaries at the time and didn't understand her energy would harm me. A flash back forced me to realize this was a powerful energy directed towards me. "Perhaps she put a hex on me?" I would recite a prayer for her so she would heal. Time for me now to heal and move on.

A few months later, dad developed the most aggressive type of prostate cancer. After coping for seven years, it was recommended to place him in hospice care. The time had come, and it would be a difficult decision.

Many memorable times occurred while my dad received hospice care. I moved in with my parents to help. There was regularly a clash between us, and I personally craved us to both heal before his passing.

"Dad, this is your parade. Keep doing what you are doing until you choose. Don't let anybody tell you when you are leaving to die. Keep going to your card games, having friends visit and everything you enjoy."

"I never thought of it that way." Dad looked at me surprised like he had no choice.

Each day his body would fade a little further. But his demand for daily smoothies would remain persistent. At the time, I was working at a nearby healthcare facility. Dad's condition worsened and he begged me not to send him to the hospital. Promising him he could stay home, I felt guilty, but he needed the care. As he repeated those words, a knife began thrusting deeper into my heart. My heart ripped open, raw.

Two days thereafter, I went to visit him. He was more alert. "I'm afraid," he said. This was "*it.*" "Dad, whatever you were taught about death; it wasn't fire, brimstone, and judgement. It's love like no other, beautiful peace, and forgiveness beyond belief." He looked away from me and shrugged his shoulders. I sensed his uncertainty. As he sank back to sleep, I prayed the angels would support him.

We gathered in the evening, as a family around my dad. I misstepped and stumbled on the floor in front of my dad's bed. The agony was so intense, I felt as though I was going to puke, and my head spun like a merry go round. They announced a code for a person down. Working at this same healthcare facility, I recognized what it meant.

Like a scene from a film, healthcare providers came rushing around the corners, up the staircases shouting orders. Despite their efforts to get me to the ER, I declared, I'm fine, as they ignored me. My knee was shattered, and the orthopedic surgeon would not be available until Monday.

Monday finally came, and I was in the surgeon's office waiting room. Lights of pink and gold began swirling above my head, and in my head. My dad's voice distinctly provided me a message he was ok. "You're right, it's nothing like I had imagined." Thy will was done.

I was so fixated on the outside world, having tasks done. The task list is irrelevant in this world once I had my own head injury. I learned to let it go. Especially since many things, including writing, would be a challenge.

It's about the people God brings into our lives. However they show up I really believe we are here to help each other along this journey on a soul level.

Not everyone is a BFF, but why are we together? To learn?

Today, I believe in divine connection–we are all part/center of God. One has no separation. Forgiveness to heal and help others is my purpose.

The love remains with me. Like an ecstasy of pure, unconditional love, in my body. An enhanced awareness of all that is good. Golden pink. Bathed by a grandmother's hug. Totally relaxed. Monkey mind turned off. Magnified awareness of nature. Everything has resonating light filled with divine love.

This is the forefront of my life now.

I truly believe there is a progression of soul and humanity. We align ourselves with the ultimate love; we are fulfilling a mission.

Listen to your soul—you are fulfilling your purpose as you walk on this earth. You will have spiritual peace.

Beauty in the light

As it transforms through my soul

Sparkling golden colors which emanate purity and love.

A fine mist makes one lose sight

I feel diminished and devoured by those who feared my power

I lost my strength and clarity when I was confused.

Protect yourself, I hear from God

For they do not want you to keep your beauty and innocence

They need it to survive.

My heart is filled with the Love of God

and that's all I need to thrive.

–Gloria Coppola

Teaka Carrasco

A mom to three amazing boys and married for 14 years to the love of her life, Rigo. Originally from Midwest Ohio, she and her family now reside on the West Coast snuggling up with their 8 rescue dogs.

Teaka is an avid horse lover and grew up in the arenas of both show and harness racing. She is a health and wellness advocate for herself and those along with her struggling with the many symptoms of rare disease. Presently, she is testing stem cell activation patches in an effort to restore body systems to normal function.

Teaka works full-time doing freelance graphic design work, and offering Virtual Assistant services to businesses in various genres. Much of her work is with Powerful Potential & Purpose Publishing, but you can find more at Carrasco Creations on Facebook.

In her spare time, you can find her hanging out with her kids, crocheting, or into anything about arts and crafts. Being in creative mode is her favorite place to be.

Email: carrascoteaka@gmail.com
FB: @CarrascoCreations
Insta: @LiveYourBestVibe
Twitter: @LiveURBestVibe
TikTok: @LiveYourBestVibe1

CHAPTER FOURTEEN

Can't Never Could

TEAKA CARRASCO

I remember the day like yesterday. I was nervously knocking my feet together, sitting on the edge of the examining table in my neurologist's office, when he read the gut-wrenching report that I had Chiari Malformation. In an instant, it hindered me carrying groceries and rendered me incapable of carrying my children to bed. A bitter and blistery January afternoon, yet the sun was shining. I had just died inside, like the leaves in the fall, to prepare for the pending cold winter. Chiari Malformation is a herniation of the cerebellum causing a variety of neurological symptoms. Numbness in my legs was my primary symptom at first, many others have headaches; I am glad I don't get those.

I recall the initial moment I answered, "I can't, I'm sorry." A friend asked me to help them move. There was this monumental sense of letdown, and an increasing emptiness brewing in the pit of my belly. It's tough to describe that feeling, and yet my 'I can't' list proceeded to mount higher, each one more devastating than the last. I was helpless.

I can't go to the amusement park with friends to ride the roller coasters anymore. I can't take a flight with a co-worker for a weekend getaway to a cabin in the splendid mountains of Tennessee. "I wish, but I can't do high elevations now."

People didn't understand it and before I realized it, I would grieve the loss of relationships with friends and people. My heart seemed vacant. A shell of what was prior, filled to the brim with love and laughter had become hollow, yet still maintaining a beat.

It was simpler to become reclusive, a prisoner in my mind and home. I didn't choose to be that person you might invite out of obligation or pity so I can reply "I can't."

In hindsight, much of my life, even prior to a life altering diagnosis, "I can't" had literally become my biggest crutch response to a lot of other parts of my life as well.

I mention this because I think of the phrase "can't, never, could" being a frequent response from my grandmother whenever I would tell her I can't. When younger, it didn't make sense to me, and I would brush it off. As I've gotten older, more so now, it definitely hits home.

My negative and critical mindset had evolved into one with huge dreams, goals, and ambitions. I would take actionable steps towards these matters, and just before the real potential might have shown through–the "I can't" consumed my mind and I would give up.

Before I realized it, I would have many wonderful things show up to transform my life for the better, but I hadn't accomplished a single one. 'I can't' had become who I was before I even recognized it. By the time of my diagnosis, I had been so programmed by my perceived inability, I undoubtedly believed that I couldn't.

Everyone else thought I had lost my mind. If I had a dollar for every friend, family member, or co-worker who'd advise me,

"You can do it, it's all in your head," I would be a millionaire. The dilemma was, *in my head*, but not in how they were perceiving it.

When I lost my father in 2018, I fell back in love with drawing and creating. I needed to escape the reality that I couldn't bring him back.

When designing, I am a magician. As a child, I recall the thousands of fashion styles I had conjured up. Creating women dresses, with pen or pencil, on any blank space of paper, I loved having fun. I discovered drawing provides me a sense of peace, of healing, and of accomplishment.

Come to think of it, there was never a moment where I couldn't, when drawing. It allowed me to be free from my way of thinking. It provided me the opportunity to express myself through pictures, and I was good at it. Playing with design granted me the courage and confidence to pursue my current role as a Virtual Assistant and graphic designer. I'd found that design had placed me in perfect alignment with many other matters, for my health and wellness as well.

Until about two years ago, I had shoved my condition under the rug. The fact that my condition was continuing to deteriorate was inevitable. I was working from home and still had my ears to hear, eyes to see, and use my hands. However, my mobility was restricted, my pain was more persistent. I had wasted more time lounging on the couch rather than moving around.

The point arrived where I couldn't. I couldn't walk long distances. I couldn't bend over without stumbling. I couldn't move around my home without purposefully having things in my path to grasp onto on my way to the bathroom, kitchen, and bedroom.

'I can't' started to show up in my parenting, in my work, in my willingness to try alternative healing methods, and in my will to fight and thrive. I had turned over the notion since they had no cure for my diagnosis, I submitted. I had all but laid down and died. I experienced, almost a sense of relief that happens with submission and the sense you don't need to fight with yourself. However, I have three children who still need their mom, so laying down was not an option.

In the midst of my madness, I reached out to my boss, who has become a best friend. She let me regurgitate all of my "I cant's" over our direct message conversation online. I mustered up all the negativity, I swear, from my 42 years of life. I ended with, "I'm just tired."

The complexity behind her response will live with me for the rest of my life. She didn't sugarcoat it or beg me to stop or urge me to follow her guidance. Direct, honest, and to the point, and I required it. The defining motivator behind why I am here now telling you my story.

"Over these years, I have provided you endless opportunities of coaching. Life coaching, health coaching. I have mailed you alternatives which you refused to try. If you don't wish your life back, then continue sitting on your hands and you will die. If you do want help, then you know what to do and you know where I am. You need to change your mindset."

At first, her response surprised me. I think for a fleeting moment, I was expecting her to beg and sugar coat, but then if I was looking for that type of response, I wouldn't have gone to her specifically. I rely on her candor and reaching out to her that day, was no mistake.

She wasn't lying either. Opportunity after opportunity pissed away because I can't. To this day, I do not perceive how she puts up with me. In a flash I finally made the choice "I can."

Every morning I wake up grateful for another day. I can change the way I use my senses, the process of praying. I can do anything I set my mind to. I can change my life.

She was kind enough to send me some stem cell regeneration therapy patches months ago. Honestly, I did not use them according to the directions; but they helped despite my stubbornness. I opened her countless emails with recipe suggestions refusing to try before now. I made them, and I enjoy them. I detected things shifting, changes in my work and also with my health. My work was more focused, better than before.

People were asking me to help them with design work all of a sudden. I was more organized and kept up with multiple tasks at once. I seemed less fatigued, more focused, and very energized.

I think sometimes in life, when you've become so detached from everybody, you tend to feel like you have to take life by the reigns on your own. To seek help and guidance means you're unloading the heaviness of your chaos onto someone else. That was against some ingrained rule created by God knows who, about keeping it to yourself.

Today, I'd be lying if I said I don't still have mobility issues. I still struggle with neurologic symptoms and pain. I don't have digestive issues now, although I still get hung up in the negative self-criticism. I undervalue my creativity in work and myself too often. Overall, it all has gotten much better. I can tell you with time, it will continue to improve if I remain consistent. Outside of adjusting my diet, this new mindset has empowered me to quit a thirty-year addiction to soda and take on extra projects with minimal issues.

Thoughts become things, and these things don't just affect the issue or situation at hand. I am understanding that even claiming "I can't wait" is part of my old habit. I've been inclined to see positive results by speaking "Looking forward to it" instead. The power in manifestation is real. Even if my intention was good, they may perceive it as a "can't." It has been and will remain to be a learning and transformational process. I am living proof that each of us carries the magnitude to heal and grow through our own intentions.

We are not meant to go at this life alone. The part about "it takes a village" isn't just about raising children. It's about raising adults too. With the right supportive people in your circle, there isn't anything that can't be accomplished.

It is easy to fall down when a perceived failure encompasses the intricacies of your mind. The get back up is what matters. The recognition that failure isn't a failure, rather, it is a guiding stone to your next destination where your accomplishment lays in waiting. Manifesting and giving all you have to your present capabilities, while leaving the can'ts behind, is going to serve you better than marinating in details you can't control.

Those many years ago, "can't, never, could" made little sense to me. At a youthful age, I'd just roll my eyes and brushed it off and my "I can'ts" were plenty.

I understand I manifested it all in my life back then. Now, I am in the process of maneuvering my way out of it. Forgiving myself for being human hasn't been the simplest but realizing there is a path out of it has created a tremendous difference.

We all have the potential to succeed, whatever success means for you, it is all within reach. We just have to feed ourselves with the can's and 'I will's' rather than I can'ts because "can't, never, could," and can't never will.

"The Pendulum of the mind oscillates between sense and nonsense, not between right and wrong."

–Carl Jung

Conclusion

A NOTE FROM GLORIA COPPOLA

I read through each story, and I am reminded of the many times in life, I journaled. The stories I told myself, the assumptions I've made and the pain I harbored within my heart.

Each author, authentically shared from places I recall when I was younger. I would like to dedicate something I wrote decades ago to each of them. May it provide encouragement and inspiration to continue their growth and finding their soul purpose.

"I am leaving soon, by myself. I feel I know who I am. Finally.
I am not afraid to taste what life has to offer.
I welcome the quiet space I have found inside.
I am alone, but not lonely. I feel loved, by me.
I breathe, I live, I love. I see, I know and believe now.
I open myself to a higher realm of power and love.
It lifts the veil of illusions.
I fear not what I now know. It is clear.
Patience, has brought me to peace.
Insights, has shown me the way.
Love, will keep me alive.
I am comfortable in knowing I no longer need to struggle. For that was never God's intent.
Thank you, Lord, for giving me/them strength and allow me/us to find our paths and destiny.

Much gratitude and love,

Gloria

GLORIA COPPOLA

Gloria Coppola specializes in helping others find their true purpose. She has endured several personal losses and overcome many challenges, including depression. These experiences led her on an inner soul journey to self love and have provided her the ability to engage and empathize with those who have lost hope.

Working along with shaman, kahuna, mentors like Bob Proctor, Gloria learned more about her unique gifts and soul purpose. It guided her to receive and align with the frequency of love. Love feeds our souls.

When Gloria isn't life coaching or helping others to write their stories, she loves to travel and host retreats. Too Many Goodbyes, her first fictional novel was inspired by her international travels.

Gloria is a visionary and award-winning author and educator, and international professional life and health coach. She received a humanitarian award for non-profit services she provided to the massage community and was inducted into the Massage Hall of Fame for her years of educational dedication. She has also been a featured writer for various holistic magazines over the years and an international speaker.

She enjoys engaging others to live a soul-driven life and empowering them to live an inspirational professional and personal life. Her soul purpose consultations are life changing for those ready to seek guidance from a higher level of consciousness and tap into the truth of their purpose.

Contact: Gloria@gloriacoppola.com
www.PPP-publishing
Facebook Gloria Coppola, author

BOOKS:

Both Ends of the rainbow
You Were Born to Love
Women Standing Strong Together Volume I
Breakthrough wisdom of the soul
The path of awakening
Awakening the consciousness of humanity
Too Many Goodbyes, a novel of adventure and love

Celebrate Life

GLORIA COPPOLA

In a quiet place deep within

I can hear so much

The answers are there if we know the

questions to ask

Allow the light to enter and fill yourself with joy

You deserve love.

Breathing in as if for the very first time

I celebrate life.

Become a Published Author!

Gloria Coppola was guided to align with heart-centered writers who have a bold, courageous, and important message for the world. She has been writing for four decades and published six of her own books along with hundreds of magazine articles.

Providing intuitive and professional attention for independent authors to publish their books; she has helped over fifty in the last four years; most who became best sellers and several who won awards.

- *Soul focused, creative writing and storytelling coaching.*
- *Receive one on one coaching with Gloria through video sessions – available option*
- *Professional publishing services. We never keep your royalties*
- *Editing and proof reading*
- *Custom design covers and interior formatting layout*
- *Competitive analysis for book placement on Amazon*
- *Marketing and book launch guidance*
- *One of a kind personal touch*
- *You keep all your rights for your novels and stories.*

Your story is needed now more than ever!
Contribute your light to the world and become
a published author NOW!

Powerful
Potential and Purpose

PUBLISHING
SERVICES

www.PPP-publishing.com

CONTACT: Gloria@Gloriacoppola.com
www.PPP-publishing.com

www.ingramcontent.com/pod-product-compliance
Lightning Source LLC
Chambersburg PA
CBHW070702130626
46553CB00005B/1807